UNLOCKING CLOSE READING

by Linda Feaman and
Nancy Geldermann

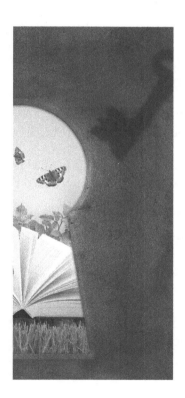

Maupin House *by*
capstone®
professional

Unlocking Close Reading
By Linda Feaman and Nancy Geldermann

© 2015. Linda Feaman and Nancy Geldermann. All rights reserved.

Cover Design: Sandra D'Antonio
Book Design: Jodi Pedersen

Image Credits:
All cover and interior images from Shutterstock

Library of Congress Cataloging-in-Publication Data
Cataloging-in-publication information is on file with the Library of Congress.

978-1-62521-928-2 (pbk.)
978-1-62521-938-1 (eBook PDF)
978-1-62521-952-7 (eBook)

Maupin House publishes professional resources for K–12 educators. Contact us for tailored, in-school training or to schedule an author for a workshop or conference.

Visit www.maupinhouse.com for free lesson plan downloads.

Maupin House Publishing, Inc. by Capstone Professional
1710 Roe Crest Drive
North Mankato, MN 56003
www.maupinhouse.com
888-262-6135
info@maupinhouse.com

Printed in the United States of America in Eau Claire, Wisconsin.
042014   008206

DEDICATION

for Scott and Jerry

TABLE OF CONTENTS

PREFACE:
A Note from the Authors

The beginnings of this book took place in the classroom. After developing the lessons and process of implementation and sharing it with teachers and administrators, the resounding response was always, "You should write a book!" This book is an answer to the request for standards-based, teacher- and student-friendly close reading lessons that are ready for use.

We often search the words of others for inspiration and to best express our own message. The following quotes encapsulate and synthesize the essence of this book and the very art and craft of teaching reading.

> "Reading without reflecting is like eating without digesting."
> —Edmund Burke

> "Reading is to the mind what exercise is to the body."
> —Sir Richard Steele

> "A writer only begins a book. A reader finishes it."
> —Samuel Johnson

> "To teach is to learn twice."
> —Joseph Joubert

So let us teach students to truly digest what they have read by exercising their minds through purposefully designed lessons. Let us learn how to help transmit what an author has to say about a topic and facilitate the transaction between the writer and the reader of the text. Finally, let us create opportunities for our students by making them capable of truly understanding what they have read.

> "Today a reader, tomorrow a leader."
> —W. Fusselman

Linda Feaman
Nancy Geldermann

INTRODUCTION:
Unlocking Close Reading

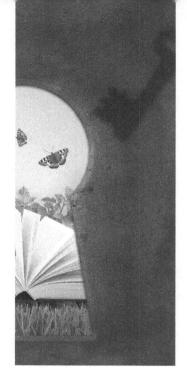

Overview

This book is intended as a guide to facilitate effective and insightful implementation of close reading. The Common Core State Standards has given educators a cohesive and complete set of expectations for instruction and learning designed to prepare students for college and career readiness. An underlying skill woven through all aspects of the Common Core is that of close reading. In fact, 80 to 90 percent of the reading standards in each grade require text dependent analysis. An essential understanding requisite is that **close reading is a transaction between the reader and the text.** Our mission then, as educators, is to teach students to read closely to uncover the true essence of what an author has to say about a given topic. The lessons in this book teach students to unlock the central idea of a passage and thus complete the transaction.

The goal of this book is to provide a better understanding of the process of close reading for teachers and administrators alike. The hardest parts of facilitating any new initiative are coming to a clear understanding of its components and becoming knowledgeable enough to implement them successfully in the classroom setting. Herein we offer a complete set of first steps to close the gap between knowing we have work to do … and knowing how to do it.

These lessons are Common Core-aligned and standards based. They are designed to move students through the rigorous process of close reading and to help them become critical thinkers capable of unlocking and extracting key meanings and ideas found within the various materials they read. Each lesson engages students in complex informational text. Text-dependent questions have been carefully designed with deliberate scaffolding to provide differentiation for all students, including those with special needs as well as second language learners.

Close reading leads students to deep, important meanings that can be found within a text worth reading. The basic components of the close-reading process include:

- Careful and purposeful rereading.
- Focusing on what the author has to say.
- Focusing on the author's point of view.
- Analyzing how the words add meaning to the text.
- Focusing on text-dependent questions that are designed to allow students to think about the structure of the text and how it impacts their understanding of it.

An important additional feature of this book is the inclusion of tools to assess student learning. It is critical to note that reading and writing in the Common Core are closely connected, and with this in mind, we have added an integral writing component. This component has been designed to assess students' understanding of what they have read and to measure their ability to move from oral to written discourse.

Each lesson includes:

- Grade-level appropriate, complex informational text for close reading
- Reproducible copy of text for students
- Teacher Discussion Guide that facilitates discussion and differentiation, which is a copy of the text that includes text-dependent questions embedded and annotated alongside the body of the student text
- Prompts designed to facilitate student writing of constructed-response paragraphs
- Teacher rubrics to drive instruction
- Exemplars designed to illustrate and further advance understanding of expected performance
- Student-friendly checklists for self-assessment, reflection, and feedback

Function of Each Section of the Book

1. Introduction: Unlocking Close Reading: explanation of close reading and the instructional process presented in the book.

2. Overview of a Close Reading Lesson: explanation of each part of the lessons included in the book.

3. Close Reading Lesson Procedure: step-by-step explanation of the lesson procedure.

4. Overview of Lesson Grade Levels and Text Complexity: scope of text complexity and suggested grade level of lessons.

5. Lessons: twelve close reading lessons that include:
   - Reproducible student texts
   - Teacher Discussion Guides
   - Writing prompts and annotated exemplars

6. Appendix: includes prewriting organizers, writing rubrics, student checklists, and glossary.

7. Master List of Capstone Mentor Texts: list of Capstone Classroom publications used as sources for student texts.

How to Use This Book

Read the Overview of a Close Reading Lesson (page 12), and then read several different student texts above and below a specific grade level to gain an understanding of the continuum of text complexity that builds from lesson to lesson. Take several things into consideration before choosing an introductory lesson: students' instructional level, students' discussion and thinking skill levels, and how to get the most use from the lessons provided in this book.

The best introductory text is one that can be read easily, but still requires high levels of cognitive demand to uncover the central idea. The goal of an introductory lesson is to introduce the thinking processes required for successful close reading. Choosing an easier text for the first lesson will help students spend their time thinking about the text rather than struggling to read it.

Starting with a text slightly below your students' grade level also provides a continuum of progressively more complex texts to use with your students in successive lessons. For example, a fourth grade class could begin with Lesson 4: *What If There Were No Sea Otters?* and, over time, work up to Lesson 7: *Medgar Evers*. Starting with a successful introductory lesson and working through the more difficult ones that follow will provide students with successive, progressive challenges that build on each other to lead them toward independence with close reading.

Kindergarten teachers can begin with Lesson 1: *Everyone Feels Angry Sometimes* using a projection of the text and a read-aloud strategy, and go as high as Lesson 3: *What Eats What in a Rain Forest Food Chain* after the thinking processes have been introduced and practiced.

Because all of the text selections were chosen for their complexity, it is our expectation that all of the texts can be used to address individual student, classroom, and professional needs. Lesson 1 can be used as the introductory lesson for kindergartens, it can be used to introduce close reading to struggling readers in the middle grades, and it can be used to introduce teachers to close reading during a professional development opportunity. After students have had time to practice close reading with several lessons at their grade level, Lesson 1 can also be used as an independent assessment to measure students' readiness to move on to doing more close reading on their own. The range of complexity of thought required for each lesson was purposely included to provide a variety of challenges for your students. Becoming familiar with lessons suggested for grade levels other than your own will extend the usefulness of this book.

OVERVIEW of a
Close Reading Lesson

Following is a general overview of the close reading lessons provided in this book. Examples of the components highlighted in **bold** reference either a specific lesson (Lesson 6: *Humpback Whales,* page 87) or the Appendix (starting on page 142).

These lessons are designed to be introductory in that they provide both the questioning and thinking necessary for close, analytical reading. The questioning is done through a teacher-facilitated whole or small group discussion during which an important central idea from the text is uncovered.

The lessons introduce critical thinking skills that are essential to close reading. The **Student Texts** (see Lesson 6: *Humpback Whales,* page 87) were chosen for their substantive content. As students gain experience with this type of lesson, they will learn to develop, ask, and answer text-dependent questions on their own. After repeated, supported practice, students will ultimately be able to transfer and apply the close reading process skills modeled in these lessons to their own independent reading of complex informational text.

The **Teacher Discussion Guides** (see Lesson 6: *Humpback Whales,* page 89) include a logical sequence of text-dependent questions that lead to predetermined central ideas. Allowing that there is usually more than one central idea in a text, the central idea for each of these lessons was chosen based on the following criteria:

- The central idea is inferential.
- The central idea is logical.
- The central idea can be adequately supported with text evidence.

To accommodate the uniqueness of individual classrooms and the students within them, the text-dependent questions provided in the Teacher Discussion Guides are scaffolded. The questions are designed to lead participants to the discovery of the purposefully chosen central idea. However, the number of questions needed to accomplish this will vary. Some teachers may use all of the questions while others may need to use only the key ones. Most will use pedagogical reasoning to adjust questioning throughout the discussion as appropriate for the level of understanding demonstrated by student response. The Teacher Discussion Guide is *not meant to be a protocol or a script.* It is meant to provide a structure that will support a vibrant, engaging discussion in your classroom.

Each lesson concludes with a **Prompt** (see Lesson 6: *Humpback Whales,* page 93) to measure both students' understanding of the text based on the discussion and their ability to demonstrate that understanding in written form. Prompts relate directly to the specified central idea and lead students to follow the logic of the discussion in their responses. **Annotated Constructed Response Exemplars** (see Lesson 6: *Humpback Whales,* page 93) are included to provide guidance for writing instruction.

The **Thought Capturer** (starting on page 150) serves as a bridge between the discussion and the written response. This organizer parallels the structure of the constructed response paragraph and can be used as a thought synthesizer as well as a prewriting tool.

Constructed Response Instructional Rubrics and **Response to Reading Checklists** (starting on page 152) are included to guide writing instruction and to help students with self-assessment.

The Common Core State Standards clearly charges educators with the mission of teaching students to read closely while interacting with multiple complex texts in order to prepare them to be successful in college and career pursuits. These lessons will help teachers facilitate the beginnings of this practice and move toward a comprehensive understanding of the skill of close reading.

CLOSE READING
Lesson Procedure

1. Initial Reading

The lesson begins with an initial reading using copies of the **Student Text.** This can be done as a read-aloud, independent silent reading, partner reading, or any other method that is effective for the students in your classroom and appropriate for the text. We recommend teacher read-alouds with projected text for younger students and teacher read-alouds with student copies of text for older readers who struggle.

The goal of the initial reading is for all students to grasp the gist of the text. A recommended sequence follows:

1. Introduce the text.
2. Explain the method of the initial reading.
3. Proceed with the initial reading.
4. Check for understanding through partner, small group, or whole group discussion.
   - Clarify any misconceptions.
   - Define any terms not pertinent to uncovering the central idea.
   - Elicit the gist of the text.

2. Discussion

Return to the beginning of the text, and initiate the discussion using the **Teacher Discussion Guide.** The facilitator should be familiar with the sequence of questions and the central idea *before* the discussion begins to accommodate a natural flow of ideas and to assure that all students benefit from the teacher modeling and shared thinking in the classroom.

- Reread sections/sentences aloud or silently.
- Facilitate the discussion by asking questions (determine which are appropriate and imperative to ensure that all students reach the same, predetermined central idea).
- Elicit answers through teacher modeled think-alouds, individual student response, pair or small group discussions followed by whole class share outs, or through previously established classroom discussion practices.

- Encourage collaborative, shared thinking throughout the discussion, remembering that the conversation needs to be grounded in the text, and the facilitator needs to maintain that focus.
- Demonstrate annotation of the text through projection or think-alouds so that students continue to do so throughout the discussion.

Conclude the discussion by verbalizing the central idea to be sure all students have access to it.

- The method of verbalization should be determined by class dynamics and clarity of the discussion.
- The language of verbalization can be any of the following or in combination:
    - In the language of the central idea provided in the Teacher Discussion Guide.
    - Paraphrased in a way that students better understand.
    - Student generated as a result of the discussion.
    - Developed by students with partners or in small groups, then shared with class.
- The articulated central idea should be posted for reinforcement.

3. Thought Capturer

The **Thought Capturer** helps students synthesize the discussion and readies them for the writing. It is designed to help students organize their thoughts in the same manner that the constructed response should be written. It is also correlated with the Constructed Response Instructional Rubric. It includes designations for capturing the following elements from the rubric:

- The answer/thesis
- Text evidence and rationale
- A synthesized conclusion
- A new idea derived from extension of the central idea

4. Written Response

A written response is included at the end of each lesson to:
- Assess student understanding of the text as a result of the facilitated discussion.
- Push cognitive follow-through by asking students to respond to a **Constructed Response Prompt.**

The provided prompts ask students to answer questions about the author's point of view (the central idea that was uncovered during the discussion) and push them beyond basic comprehension levels by asking for evidence and rationale to support their answers.

The **Constructed Response Instructional Rubrics** and **Student Checklists** and **Exemplars** outline the essential elements that should be included in student responses:
- Answer/thesis
- Text evidence to support the thesis
- Rationale to link text evidence to the thesis
- Synthesis of the argument presented
- A takeaway/new idea that comes from close analysis of the author's point of view

The lesson model prepares students to think deeply, thoroughly, and critically while reading, discussing, and responding to the text.

Note: It is important to remember that because these lessons are designed to model the kind of cognitive engagement students will eventually be able to use when reading complex informational text independently, the predetermined central idea provided (and paraphrased forms of it) is the expected answer to the prompt. It is not the only answer, but for instructional purposes, it is the correct one.

OVERVIEW of Lesson Grade Levels and Text Complexity

The chart on the following page provides the scope of the lessons as well as recommended grade levels, Guided Reading levels, and Lexile levels for the books used with each. Please note that the levels listed are suggested ones. All of the lessons use texts worth reading and contain central ideas that are substantive.

As described in the Common Core State Standards, there are three factors to consider when measuring text complexity: qualitative evaluation of the text, quantitative evaluation of the text, and matching reader to text and task. All three factors were taken into consideration when choosing the texts for the lessons in this book. Because close reading is a complex task, and text worthy of close reading characteristically contains deep levels of meaning, some of the quantitative levels listed may seem inconsistent with grade-level expectations. Knowing that the inconsistency was taken into consideration before selection of the texts assures the validity of the range, quality, and complexity of the rigorous texts that were chosen.

Do not feel constrained by the recommended levels. Start with a text that all of your students can comprehend easily and use those that follow to practice, apply, and extend the close reading skills contained and developed in each. Once students have developed close reading skills, texts at lower or higher levels can be used for assessment, to provide challenge, or to extend and apply cognitive growth in your classroom.

It is important to note that all of the lessons are thoughtful. It is recommended that you begin with the suggested identifiers, but that you also consider the topics, the prompts, the level and depth of questioning, and the inferred central idea before deciding which texts to use with your students.

Also consider using lower and higher levels of texts to provide differentiation for students with special needs and those who are second language learners.

TEXT	GRADE LEVEL	GUIDED READING LEVEL	LEXILE LEVEL
Everyone Feels Angry Sometimes	K–1	I	340L
Three Cheers for Trees!	1–2	L	640L
What Eats What in a Rain Forest Food Chain	2–3	M	620L
What If There Were No Sea Otters?	2–4	N	820L
Albert Einstein	2–4	P	not available
Humpback Whales	4–6	P	1060L
Medgar Evers	4–6	Q	800L
A Profound Legacy from *Mesopotamia*	5–6	U	1000L
Man on the Moon	5–7	W	1050L
Tomb Explorers	5–8	V	1050L
Ethics of Sports	6–8	Z	1100L
Ethics of Politics	6–8	Y	1060L

LESSONS

LESSON Overview Recap

Following is a recap of the main points of consideration for using the Teacher Discussion Guide to facilitate implementation of these lessons. For a more detailed explanation of these points and more, refer to Overview of a Close Reading Lesson on page 12.

Teacher Discussion Guide

- Become familiar with the guide before facilitation of the discussion in order to:
    1. Internalize the logical sequence of the questions to be flexible when or if students move ahead, miss a key idea, or need additional scaffolding to come to conclusions during the discussion.
    2. Shape and orchestrate collaborative student conversations.

- Work toward the central idea:
    1. Mold the discussion to reach the purposely chosen central idea.
    2. Use the provided central idea as a guide for the end point of the discussion, but paraphrase or revise its wording to fit the language of your classroom.
    3. Give all students access to the central idea by posting it at the end of the discussion.

- Make it your own:
    1. Use the initial reading of the text to check for understanding and to clarify any relevant questions before beginning the second, more analytical reading.
    2. Avoid viewing the Teacher Discussion Guide as script. Instead, use it as a structure to guide the discussion.
    3. Use scaffolded questions to differentiate for various learning styles and capabilities.
    4. Use as many questions as are necessary to reach the synthesized central idea, being alert to the ebb and flow of the discussion.
    5. Understand that the language provided in the Teacher Discussion Guide is intended for teacher clarification. Paraphrase and use language appropriate for your students during the discussion facilitation.

6. Remember it is a guide to facilitate discussion, not a script to elicit answers. Answers included in the annotations provide: background information for the teacher; definition of terms not pertinent to discovering the central idea embedded in the lesson; and scaffolded, logical questions intended to lead to the predetermined central idea.

- Stay grounded in the text:
   1. Focus the discussion and questioning on what the author has to say.
   2. Push students back into the text to find evidence to support their reasoning.
   3. Model and encourage annotation of the text.

- Identify key vocabulary ahead of time:
   1. Words related to the central idea should be defined through context clues or word-part analysis as noted in the Teacher Discussion Guide.
   2. Words unrelated to the central idea and/or key concepts needed before reading should be defined or explained by the teacher as noted in the Teacher Discussion Guide.

Discussion Management

- Use established discussion procedures and configurations that work in your classroom.
- Vary the turn and talks, partner, and small group interactions to involve all students in collaborative conversation throughout the course of the discussion.
- Use the share out to:
   1. Check for understanding.
   2. Mold the conversation.
   3. Clarify misconceptions.
   4. Suggest new ideas that students are struggling to uncover.

Everyone Feels Angry Sometimes

by Cari Meister

1

Everyone has feelings.

Sometimes people feel happy.

Other times people feel sad.

People can feel angry or scared too.

These feelings are normal.

2

Sofie's dog chewed her new shoes.

Sofie feels like her head will explode!

Sofie talks to her mom.

They find a better place to keep her other shoes.

3

Trevin is building an airplane.

His sister breaks off the wing.

Trevin throws the airplane into the trash can.

Trevin needs time to calm down.

He goes for a run.

Mr. Sanchez keeps a garden.

Mateo bikes over a row of flowers.

Mr. Sanchez yells at Mateo, "Look what you have done!"

Mateo tells Mr. Sanchez he is sorry.

Together they fix the garden.

5

Isabel wants to be the star in the play.

Her teacher gives the part to Madison.

Isabel's face feels warm.

She starts to cry.

At home, Isabel sings her favorite song.

The song makes her feel better.

Jacob's mom is on the phone, and she isn't listening to him.

Jacob yells louder and louder.

"Mom!"

Jacob's mom tells him he is being rude.

Jacob plays with clay while his mom talks.

There are many ways to show anger.

There are many ways to feel less angry too.

Everyone Feels Angry Sometimes:
TEACHER DISCUSSION GUIDE

Grade Level: K–1, Guided Reading Level: I, Lexile Level: 340L

1

ᴬEveryone has feelings.

ᴮSometimes people feel happy.

Other times **ᶜ**people feel sad.

People can feel angry or **ᴰ**scared too.

ᴱThese feelings are normal.

2

ᶠSofie's dog chewed her new shoes.

Sofie feels like her head will explode!

ᴳSofie talks to her mom.

ᴴThey find a better place to keep her other shoes.

Ⓐ 1. Who has feelings? *Everyone; elicit that this means all ages, genders, etc.*

2. Name some different kinds of feelings. *Accept reasonable answers.*

Ⓑ 3. What makes people feel happy? *Accept reasonable answers.*

Ⓒ 4. What makes people feel sad? *Accept reasonable answers.*

Ⓓ 5. What makes people feel scared? *Accept reasonable answers.*

6. How can people feel all of these different feelings? *They don't happen all at once, nor all of the time. They come and go throughout the day and can also come in combination.*

7. Have you ever felt mad and sad at the same time? *Turn and talk. Share one example that illustrates the combined feeling.*

Ⓔ 8. What does *normal* mean? *Elicit or define: what most people do.*

9. What does the author mean when she writes that feelings are normal? *Everyone has them, and everyone experiences them. They are part of all our daily lives.*

Ⓕ 10. If Sofie is feeling like *her head will explode,* how is she feeling? *Angry*

11. What made Sofie feel like her head would explode? *The dog chewed her new shoes.*

12. Why did that make Sofie angry? *If the dog chewed her new shoes, he probably damaged them. She was mad about the shoes being damaged, but she was also mad that the dog had ruined her <u>new</u> shoes—shoes she had just received.*

Ⓖ 13. Why did Sofie talk to her mom? *To get help with her anger, to get help with the problem*

Ⓗ 14. What solution did Sofie and her mom come up with to prevent her other shoes from being damaged by the dog? *They found a better place to keep her other shoes.*

15. What kind of place would be a *better* place to keep her other shoes? *A place where the dog couldn't reach them: a closet, a shelf, a shoe holder, a box, etc.*

3

(I) Trevin is building an airplane.

His sister breaks off the wing.

(J) Trevin throws the airplane into the trash can.

(K) Trevin needs time to calm down.

(L) He goes for a run.

4

(M) Mr. Sanchez keeps a garden.

(N) Mateo bikes over a row of flowers.

(O) Mr. Sanchez yells at Mateo, "Look what you have done!"

(P) Mateo tells Mr. Sanchez he is sorry.

(Q) Together they fix the garden.

(I) 16. What kind of airplane was Trevin building? *A model airplane*

(J) 17. How did Trevin feel after his sister broke off the wing? How do you know? *He was angry. He threw the whole model in the trash can.*

18. Why did Trevin throw his model airplane in the trash? *He was angry about his sister breaking off the wing. He threw the model in the trash can to release some of his anger.*

(K) 19. What does it mean to *calm down? Find a way to not feel angry anymore*

20. Why would Trevin need to calm down? *He threw away his airplane, which showed he acted without thinking because he was angry. He didn't want to act out again—he wanted to calm down and get rid of his anger in a better way.*

(L) 21. Why did Trevin go for a run? *To help him get rid of his anger*

22. How would running help Trevin get rid of his anger? *It would help him release some of the anger and get it out of his system.*

23. How did Trevin deal with his anger? *Turn and talk. Elicit that at first he acted out of anger, and then he let off steam by going for a run.*

24. How was the way Trevin dealt with his anger different from the way Sofie did? *She sought help from her mother; he worked it out on his own.*

(M) 25. What does it mean to *keep a garden? It was his; he planted it, and he took care of it.*

(N) 26. What does *bikes* mean? *He rode his bike.*

27. What did Mateo do to the flowers? *He squashed them when he rode over them with his bike.*

(O) 28. Why did Mr. Sanchez yell at Mateo? *He wanted him to see what his bike riding had done to the flowers.*

29. How did Mr. Sanchez feel? How do you know? *He was angry. He was yelling to get the anger out and to stop Mateo from doing more damage.*

(P) 30. Why did Mateo tell Mr. Sanchez he was sorry? *He felt bad about squashing the flowers.*

31. What was Mr. Sanchez's response to Mateo's apology? *He forgave him.*

32. How do you know? *Mateo and Mr. Sanchez fixed the garden together. Mr. Sanchez would not have wanted to work with Mateo if he was still mad at him.*

33. How did Mr. Sanchez deal with his anger? *He let it out by yelling, and then calmed down and forgave Mateo after the apology.*

34. How was the way Mr. Sanchez dealt with his anger different from the way Sofie and Trevin did? *Elicit that he yelled to release his anger, and then made up with Mateo by working with him to fix the garden.*

(Q) 35. Why did Mateo help Mr. Sanchez fix the garden? *He was showing that his apology was real or sincere. He wanted to make up for his mistake: He wasn't just saying he was sorry, his actions showed how sorry he was.*

5

R Isabel wants to be the star in the play.

S Her teacher gives the part to Madison.

T Isabel's face feels warm.

U She starts to cry.

V At home, Isabel sings her favorite song.

The song makes her feel better.

6

W Jacob's mom is on the phone, and she isn't listening to him.

Jacob yells louder and louder.

"Mom!"

X Jacob's mom tells him he is being rude.

Y Jacob plays with clay while his mom talks.

R 36. What is a *play? A performance for an audience*

37. What is the *star* of a play? *The main character*

S 38. Where was the play being performed? *At school*

39. How do you know? *Isabel's teacher was involved.*

40. What does *part* mean in this sentence? *A part in a play; a role played by an actor*

41. Who is Madison? *A classmate*

42. What did the teacher give to Madison? *The starring role in the play that Isabel wanted*

T 43. Why did Isabel's face feel warm? *She was so sad about not getting the part that she wanted. Her face became warm as she started to cry.*

U 44. Why did Isabel start to cry? *She was feeling a different kind of anger. She was angry and disappointed at the same time, which made her feel sad.*

V 45. How did singing a favorite song make Isabel feel better? *The song made her feel better because it took her mind off not getting the part.*

46. How was the way Isabel dealt with her anger different from the way the others did? *Isabel's anger was mixed with another emotion—disappointment—which made her cry. Then she let it out in a positive way by singing a song that made her happy.*

W 47. Why did Jacob yell louder and louder? *He was trying to get his mother's attention, but she was talking to someone on the phone and ignoring him.*

48. How was Jacob feeling? How do you know? *He was angry because his mother wouldn't give him her attention, so he yelled her name over and over again.*

X 49. How did Jacob's mom react to his anger? *She told him he was being rude.*

50. What is rude behavior? *Impolite, bad behavior*

51. What did Jacob do that was rude? *He interrupted his mother while she was talking on the phone.*

Y 52. Why did Jacob play with his clay while his mom continued talking? *Turn and talk. Accept reasonable answers based on text evidence, such as: to occupy his time while he waited for his mother, to release his anger by doing something else, to change his behavior and wait for his mother's attention.*

There are many ways to show anger.

There are many ways to feel less angry too.

Z 53. Create a three-column chart like the one on page 32. With students, chart each of the characters who were angry, and how they dealt with their anger.

54. What were the different ways the characters dealt with, or got rid of, their anger? *Elicit that some let it out and some kept it in, some sought help from others, some dealt with it alone, some chose physical activities, others chose quieter ways of dealing with their anger.*

55. What did the author really want us to know about feeling angry? *Turn and talk, and then chart student responses including: Everybody gets angry, everyone has feelings, feelings are different and can happen at any time, having feelings is normal, something triggers a feeling, feelings can be expressed differently by different people, feelings can be dealt with, people feel angry sometimes—and that's OK.*

CENTRAL IDEA: People can learn different ways of dealing with anger.

Everyone Feels Angry Sometimes:
RESPONSE TO READING

Create the three-column chart, add headings, and then fill in the information with students.

Name of Angry Person	How He or She Showed Anger	What He or She Did to Feel Less Angry
Sofie	She didn't show her anger; the author tells us that she felt like her head would explode.	She talked to her mom and then found a safer place for her other shoes.
Trevin	He threw his model into the trash.	He went for a run to calm down.
Mr. Sanchez	He yelled at Mateo.	He forgave Mateo, and they fixed the garden together.
Isabel	She cried.	She sang her favorite song.
Jacob	He yelled at his mother.	He found something to do until his mother was available.

Note: This chart should be available for use with the student-written response. Two response sheets have been included. It is recommended that the first, requiring drawing only, be used for kindergarten students. The second, with fill-in-the-blank sentences plus a drawing, is recommended for first grade. You may also use both if deemed appropriate.

Directions for student-written response on following pages:

Kindergarten response (page 33): Have students choose one character from the chart to think about. Have them draw how the character showed his or her anger in the box on the left and what the character did to feel less angry in the box on the right.

First grade response (page 34): Have students choose a character from the chart to think about, then ask them to fill in the blanks to make the sentences true. Then have students draw a picture of what the character did to feel less angry.

Everyone Feels Angry Sometimes: Name: _____
RESPONSE TO READING

How was the anger shown?	What helped the anger go away?

Everyone Feels Angry Sometimes:
RESPONSE TO READING

Name:_____

1 _____ was angry because _____

_____.

2 _____ showed anger by _____

_____.

3 _____ found a way to feel less angry by

_____.

Draw a picture of what _____ did to feel less angry.

Three Cheers for Trees!
by Angie Lepetit

1

Every step you take on a beach leaves behind a footprint. So do wet steps on a dry sidewalk or a trek through a muddy yard. Your footprints change the places that you go. But what does a carbon footprint do?

2

A carbon footprint doesn't look like a foot. In fact, you can't see it at all! But it IS a mark you leave behind. A carbon footprint measures how much you change Earth by using its fossil fuel energy.

3

Coal, oil, and natural gas are fossil fuels. They are found deep inside Earth. They have given us energy for many years. But once we use them up, they will be gone forever.

4

When fossil fuels are burned for energy, they give off pollution. The pollution acts like a blanket around Earth. When the blanket thickens, Earth gets hot.

5

A hot, polluted planet isn't good for anyone. That's why we need to make good choices about our energy use. The smaller our carbon footprints, the healthier we keep Earth.

6

It takes energy to make stuff. An easy way to shrink your carbon footprint is to reuse items. Old socks can be made into puppets. Empty jelly jars make great piggy banks. By reusing items, we keep factories from making too much stuff. It keeps Earth clean too!

7

Another way to reuse old items is to give them away. Clothes you've outgrown can be given to someone else. So can bikes and shoes. Can you think of other examples?

8

If you can't reuse old items, it's time to recycle. Put glass, metal, plastic, and paper into bins. Many places will collect them. It's that easy!

9

A big part of our carbon footprint comes from driving. Cars, buses, and trucks add a lot of pollution to the air. You can keep Earth cooler and cleaner by walking or riding your bike.

10

Lights off! You can reduce your carbon footprint by using less electricity at home. Remember to turn off lights and TVs when they're not in use. In the summer, ask an adult if you can turn up the thermostat a few degrees to use less air conditioning. In the winter, turn it down to use less heat.

11

There is something else that can help us use less energy. Can you guess what? TREES! In summer, trees shade our homes and keep them cool. In winter, trees help keep our homes warm by blocking cold winds.

12

Trees are also needed to clean the air. They suck up the gas that makes Earth hot. Then trees give us oxygen to breathe. When too much gas is put in the air, trees can't keep up. This is why we need to use fewer fossil fuels. One tree makes enough oxygen for two people to breathe. Let's plant more trees!

13

Trees preserve life. Without them Earth would overheat. And we'd have nothing to breathe! Let's be mindful of what we use and do to take care of our planet. A smaller carbon footprint means a happier home for us all.

Three Cheers for Trees!:
TEACHER DISCUSSION GUIDE

Grade Level: 1–2, Guided Reading Level: L, Lexile Level: 640L

1

Every step you take on a beach leaves behind a **ⓐ**footprint. **ⓑ**So do wet steps on a dry sidewalk or a trek through a muddy yard. Your footprints **ⓒ**change the places that you go. **ⓓ**But what does a carbon footprint do?

2

ⓔA carbon footprint doesn't look like a foot. In fact, you can't see it at all! But it IS a mark you leave behind. A carbon footprint measures how much you change Earth by using its fossil fuel energy.

ⓐ 1. What is a *footprint? A mark you make when you walk on something*

ⓑ 2. What's the difference between wet footprints left in something mushy like sand or mud and those footprints left on something hard like a sidewalk? *They stay for different amounts of time. Sand and mud hold prints until they are erased by wind or water. Wet footprints on a sidewalk disappear when they dry up.*

ⓒ 3. How do footprints change the places you go? *They leave a mark that may stay for a minute or much longer, but they still leave a mark that changes what was there before you came.*

ⓓ 4. *Explain that the author doesn't expect this question to be answered at this point in the text. It was included as an introduction to what follows. Challenge students to focus on finding the answer while rereading the next four paragraphs.*

ⓔ 5. How can you leave a mark that can't be seen? *Have students turn and talk. Accept reasonable answers or provide examples such as: when you hurt someone with your words, when you break a promise, or when you do the right thing the mark is left deep inside.*

6. What is a *carbon footprint? The measure of how much you change Earth by using its fossil fuels*

7. Why can't we see our carbon footprints? *Because like the mark we leave when we hurt someone's feelings, the carbon footprint is left deep inside Earth from where the fossil fuels are taken.*

3

F"Coal, oil, and natural gas are fossil fuels. They are found deep inside Earth. They have given us energy for many years. But once we use them up, they will be gone forever.

4

When fossil fuels are burned for energy, they give off pollution. The pollution acts like a blanket around Earth. When the blanket thickens, Earth gets hot.

5

A hot, polluted planet isn't good for anyone. That's why we need to make good choices about our energy use. The smaller our carbon footprints, the healthier we keep Earth.

F 8. *Read paragraphs 3–5 aloud and explain that a diagram will help show what fossil fuels are and how they relate to our carbon footprint. See* Three Cheers for Trees! *Diagram on page 47.*

9. *Draw the diagram using language from the text to explain as you draw. Start with the inner circle and label it* Earth. *Add shading in center and label it* Fossil Fuel Energy *with* coal, oil, and natural gas *listed beneath. Add flames to indicate the fossil fuels burning to create energy. Add rising smoke above the flames, then add the outer circle. Label it* Blanket of Pollution. *Next add the stick figure. Include droplets of sweat, a sad face, and the dialogue bubble.*

10. How would a smaller carbon footprint keep Earth healthier? *Elicit or explain: A smaller footprint would mean using less fossil fuel energy. That would mean less pollution and a thinner, cooler blanket of air around Earth. Earth would be healthier because it wouldn't be as polluted nor as warm as it would with a bigger footprint.*

11. *Revisit the question from the end of paragraph 1. Encourage a turn and talk, then reiterate that it leaves an invisible mark on Earth because it is a measure of how much fossil fuel energy each person uses up. We can't see the fossil fuels because they are deep within Earth. What we can see is polluted air and warmer temperatures that come from burning up the fossil fuels.*

6

It takes energy to make stuff. An easy way to shrink your carbon footprint is to reuse items. Old socks can be made into puppets. Empty jelly jars make great piggy banks. By reusing items, we keep factories from making too much stuff. It keeps Earth clean too!

7

Another way to reuse old items is to give them away. Clothes you've outgrown can be given to someone else. So can bikes and shoes. Can you think of other examples?

8

If you can't reuse old items, it's time to recycle. Put glass, metal, plastic, and paper into bins. Many places will collect them. It's that easy!

G 12. What does this mean? *Factories use energy to make products.*

H 13. What does the word *reuse* mean? *Elicit or define: to use again.*

I 14. How are these examples of *reusing* things? *Items that are old or empty are being made into new things and reused for different purposes..*

J 15. How does reusing things keep factories from making too much stuff? *If people make puppets from old socks, they won't buy factory-made ones, so factories will stop making puppets. The same would be true for piggy banks.*

K 16. How does reusing things help keep Earth clean? *If factories make fewer products, they use less energy and reduce the amount of pollution released.*

L 17. How is this type of reusing different from making puppets out of old socks? *This type of reusing is different from making puppets because a person would be reusing the item in the same way as the previous owner rather than reusing it for a different purpose.*

18. How does this type of reusing help Earth? *If people reuse other people's old things, they won't have to buy new things, and factories won't have to make as many replacements.*

M 19. Can you think of other things that can be reused this way? *Turn and talk, then share. Accept reasonable answers.*

20. How does reusing shrink our carbon footprint? *Reusing things in either way decreases the need to buy factory-produced items, which means factories aren't making as much "stuff" and consequently will use less energy. Less energy use means a smaller carbon footprint.*

N 21. What does the word *recycle* mean? *Elicit or define: to reprocess something that has been used so that it can be remade and used again.*

O 22. Why would we put these things into bins? *Elicit or explain that these are bins that hold items to be recycled until they are collected.*

23. How does recycling reduce our carbon footprint? *If glass, metal, plastic, and paper are recycled, more of these items are not being made. It takes less energy to recycle them than to make new things from scratch.*

9

A big part of our carbon footprint comes from driving. Cars, buses, and trucks **ᴾ**add a lot of pollution to the air. You can keep Earth cooler and cleaner by **ᵠ**walking or riding your bike.

10

Lights off! You can **ᴿ**reduce your carbon footprint by using less electricity at home. Remember to turn off lights and TVs when they're not in use. In the summer, ask an adult if you can turn up the thermostat a few degrees to use less air conditioning. In the winter, turn it down to use less heat.

11

There is something else that can help us use less energy. Can you guess what? **ˢ**TREES! In summer, trees shade our homes and keep them cool. In winter, trees help keep our homes warm by blocking cold winds.

ᴾ 24. What kind of fossil fuel is used in cars, buses, and trucks? *Oil in the form of gasoline*

ᵠ 25. Why would walking or riding your bike keep Earth cooler and cleaner? *No fossil fuels are used when you walk or ride a bike.*

ᴿ 26. What does the word *reduce* mean? *Elicit or define: to make smaller or lessen.*

27. How can reducing the amount of electricity used reduce your carbon footprint? *Most electricity is produced by burning fossil fuels so if you're not using electricity or if you're reducing the amount you typically use, you're reducing your carbon footprint. Note: This can be inferred but may need to be explained.*

28. How does reducing (either car or electricity use) help shrink our carbon footprint? *In both cases, less use means a reduction in fossil fuel burning, which reduces the carbon footprint.*

ˢ 29. Why is this so surprising? *All of the previous suggestions have been things that people can do. Trees are plants that grow naturally on Earth.*

30. How do trees help us use less energy? *They decrease the amount of heating and cooling we need for our homes, and consequently decrease the amount of energy we use.*

12

Trees are also needed to clean the air. They suck up the gas that makes Earth hot. Then trees give us oxygen to breathe. When too much gas is put in the air, trees can't keep up. This is why we need to use fewer fossil fuels. One tree makes enough oxygen for two people to breathe. **T** Let's plant more trees!

13

Trees **U** preserve life. Without them Earth would overheat. And we'd have nothing to breathe! Let's be **V** mindful of what we use and do to take care of our planet. **W** A smaller carbon footprint means a happier home for us all.

T 31. *After reading this aloud, go back to the diagram. Add two trees and two more people. Show the trees taking in polluted air and pushing out oxygen for the two new people to breathe. Add more pollution to the air and four more people with sad faces near the tree.*

32. When there is too much pollution or gas in the air, the trees can't keep up. What could we do to help? *Elicit: "Plant more trees!"*

33. How do trees help us shrink our carbon footprint? *They help us conserve energy, and they clean the air.*

U 34. What does *preserve* mean? *Elicit or define: to protect.*

35. How do trees preserve life? *They help keep Earth from overheating, and they provide oxygen for us to breathe.*

36. What different kinds of life do trees preserve? *Turn and talk. Elicit life on Earth for all living things (plants and animals), life for the animals and plants that need oxygen (all the people on Earth), and life for us individually (each of us).*

V 37. What does *mindful* mean? *Elicit or define: to be aware of and thoughtful about.*

38. Who should be mindful of how we take care of our planet? *All of us*

39. How can we be mindful about shrinking our carbon footprint? *Turn and talk. Accept reasonable answers based on text evidence, but elicit that each of us has our own footprint, and we have to decide how to make ours as small as we can.*

W 40. How can each of us make a happier home for everyone and every animal on Earth? *By being mindful of the size of our carbon footprints*

41. *Refer to the title.* What does it mean give to three cheers for something? *To give high praise or appreciation for by shouting*

42. Why are we cheering trees? *Because they preserve our lives and the lives of everyone and everything on the planet just by living. They work to keep both us and our planet healthy without even being asked! We are also cheering to thank them and show our appreciation for what they do.*

43. What is the author telling us about our carbon footprint? *We should work as hard as the trees do to preserve life on Earth.*

CENTRAL IDEA: We need to reuse, recycle, reduce, and preserve to keep life healthy on Earth.

Three Cheers for Trees!:
DIAGRAM

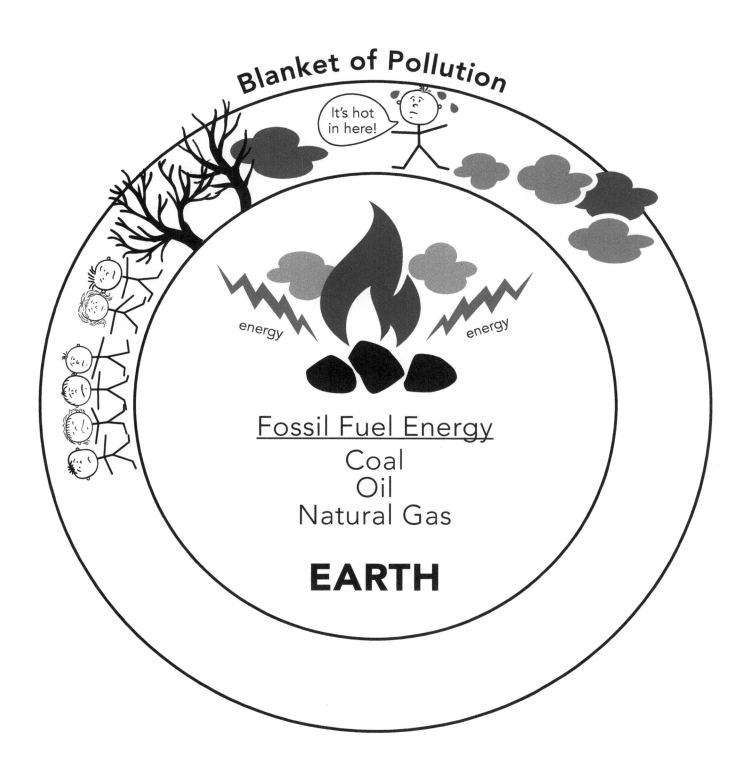

Three Cheers for Trees!:
RESPONSE TO READING

Name: _____

Draw a picture of yourself helping Earth in each of the following ways. Then complete the sentence below using the Word Bank to help you.

REUSE	RECYCLE	REDUCE	PRESERVE

If we _____ the amount of _____

we use, we can _____ our carbon footprint

so that _____ on Earth is a happy and healthy

home for _____ .

Three Cheers for Trees!: ANSWER KEY

Recommended for Grade 1

Draw a picture of yourself helping Earth in each of the following ways. Then complete the sentence below using the Word Bank to help you.

Note: Answers may vary, but should show pictures of the student helping the planet.

REUSE	RECYCLE	REDUCE	PRESERVE

WORD BANK:
shrink   all
decrease
fossil fuels   life

If we <u>decrease</u> the amount of <u>fossil fuels</u>

we use, we can <u>shrink</u> our carbon footprint

so that <u>life</u> on Earth is a happy and healthy

home for <u>all</u>.

Three Cheers for Trees!:
RESPONSE TO READING

Name: _____

Explain how you can use each of these methods to shrink the carbon footprint.
Use text evidence in your answers.

METHOD	EXAMPLE	RESULT
REUSE		
RECYCLE		
REDUCE		
PRESERVE		

What is the author really saying about shrinking <u>your</u> carbon footprint?

_____

_____

_____

_____

Three Cheers for Trees!:
ANSWER KEY

Recommended for Grade 2

Explain how you can use each of these methods to shrink the carbon footprint.
Use text evidence in your answers.

METHOD	EXAMPLE	RESULT
REUSE	Use an old sock to make a puppet.	The factory won't need to make new puppets, which will save energy by reducing the amount of fossil fuel burned. The less fossil fuel used, the smaller the carbon footprint will be.
RECYCLE	Recycle glass, metal, plastic, and paper.	Recycling uses less energy than making any of these things from scratch. Using less energy shrinks the carbon footprint.
REDUCE	Turn off the lights when I don't need them.	Using less electricity means using less energy, which helps to reduce my carbon footprint.
PRESERVE	Plant three trees! Hip, hip, hooray!	Trees clean up the air that makes Earth hot, and they also give me oxygen to breathe. I could plant one tree to help preserve Earth, but I'd rather plant three so that I can help people other than me!

What is the author really saying about shrinking your carbon footprint?

It is up to me to help everyone on Earth by shrinking my own carbon footprint. The author wants me to know that the choices I make every day affect our planet in every way.

What Eats What in a Rain Forest Food Chain

by Lisa J. Amstutz

1

From a chirping katydid to a hungry jaguar, all living things in a rain forest are part of a food chain. Each living thing in a food chain eats the one before it.

2

Almost all food chains rely on the sun. In the rain forest, the sun shines down on the silky leaves of a cacao tree, which is a producer. Producers use sunlight, water, nutrients, and air to make their own food.

3

A katydid nibbles the cacao leaf. This insect is hard to spot. Its green wings look like a leaf. It is a consumer. Consumers eat plants or animals for energy. An herbivore eats only plants.

4

A hungry tree frog sees the katydid move. ZAP! He shoots out his long, sticky tongue. What a tasty snack for a tree frog! A carnivore eats only other animals.

5

The tree frog blends in with the leaves. But a blue-crowned motmot eyes it after eating some berries. The bird snatches the frog. An omnivore eats both plants and animals.

6

An emerald tree boa hangs from a branch. When the motmot flies by, the snake makes its move.

7

A jaguar is hungry. It stalks the snake … climbs the tree … and pounces!

8

The jaguar is a powerful hunter, but it doesn't live forever. One day the jaguar has a deadly fall. A king vulture finds the cat's body and feeds. A scavenger eats mainly dead plants or animals.

9

Insects, bacteria, and fungi feed on what's left of the jaguar's body. Decomposers break down dead plants and animals. Their waste is used as nutrients by plants.

10

Nutrients from the jaguar's body will return to the soil. In spring a new cacao tree will grow in this soil. And the food chain will continue.

Note: Begin the lesson by asking students what a chain is. Elicit that it is a sequence of interlocking links, and then have students line up to form a human chain by interlocking their elbows.

The chain should be linear at this point. Once students understand the concept, have them return to their seats for the close reading discussion.

What Eats What in a Rain Forest Ⓐ*Food Chain:*
TEACHER DISCUSSION GUIDE

Grade Level: 2–3, Guided Reading Level: M, Lexile Level: 620L

1

From a chirping katydid to a hungry jaguar, Ⓑall living things in a rain forest are part of a food chain. ⒸEach living thing in a food chain eats the one before it.

2

Almost all food chains Ⓓrely on the sun. In the rain forest, Ⓔthe sun shines down on the silky leaves of a cacao tree, which is a producer. ⒻProducers use sunlight, water, nutrients, and air to make their own food.

3

A Ⓖkatydid nibbles the cacao leaf. This insect is hard to spot. Its green wings look like a leaf. It is a consumer. ⒽConsumers eat plants or animals for energy. An Ⓘherbivore eats only plants.

Ⓐ 1. What is a *food chain? Elicit or say: A sequence that shows how each living thing in an ecosystem gets its food, and how nutrients and energy are passed from living thing to living thing.*

Ⓑ 2. What is a *living thing? Encourage a turn and talk with a partner. During share out, elicit that living things require energy (food) to live. Facilitate the discussion by charting examples and nonexamples. Be sure to include both plants and animals.*

Ⓒ 3. What does this mean? *A food chain is a sequence that passes food energy necessary for life from living thing to living thing. "The one before it" would be the plant or animal that is eaten.*

Ⓓ 4. What does *rely* mean? *Elicit from context clues or define: to be dependent on, to need.*

5. Why do food chains rely on the sun? *Because all food chains begin with plants, and plants need the sun to produce their own food.*

Ⓔ 6. What happens when the sun shines on the cacao leaves? *The plant produces its own food for energy to live.*

Ⓕ 7. What are *producers? Living things that produce their own food (plants)*

Ⓖ 8. What kind of an animal is a katydid? *An insect*

9. How do you know? *Elicit that the answer is in the next sentence.*

Ⓗ 10. What is a *consumer? An animal that eats plants or animals for energy*

11. How is a consumer different from a producer? *A producer makes its own food for energy, and a consumer consumes or eats plants and animals to get its energy to live.*

Ⓘ 12. What is an *herbivore? A consumer that eats only plants*

13. Is a katydid an herbivore? How do you know? *It is. It eats cacao leaves for energy to live.*

4

J A hungry tree frog sees the katydid move. ZAP! He shoots out his long, sticky tongue. What a tasty snack for a tree frog! A **K** carnivore eats only other animals.

5

The **L** tree frog blends in with the leaves. But a **M** blue-crowned motmot eyes it after eating some berries. **N** The bird snatches the frog. An **O** omnivore eats both plants and animals.

6

An **P** emerald tree boa hangs from a branch. When the motmot flies by, the snake **Q** makes its move.

7

A jaguar is hungry. It **R** stalks the snake **S** ... climbs the tree ... and **T** pounces!

J 14. What does the tree frog do to the katydid? *The tree frog eats the katydid.*

K 15. What is a *carnivore? An animal that eats only other animals.*

16. Is the tree frog a carnivore? How do you know? *It is. It eats the katydid for energy to live.*

L 17. How does the tree frog blend in? *It is green like the leaves so it is hard to distinguish.*

M 18. What kind of animal is a motmot? *A bird*

19. How do you know? *Elicit that the context clue is in the next sentence.*

20. What does *eyes* mean? *Watching with interest*

N 21. What happened to the frog? *The bird ate it.*

O 22. What is an *omnivore? An animal that eats both plants and animals*

23. Is the motmot an omnivore? How do you know? *It is. It eats berries (plant) and the frog (animal) for energy.*

P 24. What kind of an animal is an emerald tree boa? *It is a snake.*

25. How do you know? *Elicit that the answer is in the next sentence.*

Q 26. What "move" does the snake make? *It catches and eats the motmot.*

R 27. What does *stalks* mean? *Follow, sneak up on, track down*

28. Why is the jaguar stalking the snake? *The jaguar is hungry and wants to eat the snake.*

S 29. Why does the author use this type of punctuation? *It (ellipsis) indicates a pause in the sentence that replicates what the jaguar is doing—pausing as it carefully approaches the snake.*

T 30. What does *pounce* mean? *To spring forward quickly in order to catch something*

31. Why did the jaguar pounce? *To catch the snake before it could get away*

32. What happened to the snake? *The jaguar ate it.*

33. What do consumers have to do in order to catch their prey? *Turn and talk. Have students review the actions of the predators, then share out. Elicit that they have to wait and watch for the animals in order to catch them.*

8

The jaguar is a **U**powerful hunter, but it **V**doesn't live forever. One day the jaguar has a **W**deadly fall. A king vulture finds the **X**cat's body and feeds. A **Y**scavenger eats mainly dead plants or animals.

9

ZInsects, bacteria, and fungi feed on what's left of the jaguar's body. Decomposers break down dead plants and animals. Their waste is used as nutrients by plants.

U 34. What makes it a powerful hunter? *Elicit or provide an answer: It is at the top of the food chain. It can easily hunt other animals because it is big and powerful, and it survives more easily than other animals because it doesn't have many predators.*

V 35. Why doesn't the jaguar live forever? *All animals have life cycles and eventually die. If they are not consumed in the food chain, they may die naturally or by accident.*

W 36. What happened to the jaguar? *The jaguar died when it fell.*

X 37. Whose body did the vulture find? *The jaguar's body*

38. Why did the author call the jaguar a *cat? Elicit or explain: Jaguars are part of the big cat family along with lions and tigers.*

Y 39. What is a *scavenger? An animal that eats mainly dead plants or animals*

40. How are scavengers different from consumers? *Consumers have to catch and kill their prey; scavengers eat animals and plants that are already dead.*

41. Is the king vulture a scavenger? How do you know? *It is. It ate the dead jaguar.*

Z 42. *This may be a difficult paragraph for students to understand. Define* decomposers *as animals and plants that break down dead plants and animals to get food energy to live. Then elicit or explain that insects, bacteria, and fungi get their food energy from dead plants and animals because they are decomposers. Decomposers help the food chain by helping return nutrients to the soil.*

43. What are *nutrients? Food energy that comes from dead plants and animals*

44. Why do plants need nutrients? *To grow and be healthy*

10

Nutrients from the jaguar's body will
ⒶⒶ return to the soil. In spring a new
ⒷⒷ cacao tree will grow in this soil. And
the food **ⒼⒼ** chain will continue.

ⒶⒶ 45. How do nutrients return to the soil? *They sink into the ground.*

ⒷⒷ 46. What will help the new cacao tree grow? *The nutrients in the soil*

ⒼⒼ 47. How will the food chain continue? *Ask students to think back to the chain they created at the beginning of the lesson. Remind them that it was a line with a beginning and an end. Point out that the chain could not continue if there was an end to it. To demonstrate the continuation of the chain, ask students to create the chain again, but this time, send students up a few at a time as producers, consumers, scavengers, and decomposers in the order described in the text. Turn the line into a circle by reminding students that the nutrients in the soil come from the decomposers. Have the decomposers link arms with the producers to form a circular chain and to demonstrate how the chain will continue. Explain that the cacao tree will start the cycle all over again by producing its own food, which will provide food for herbivores that provide food for carnivores and omnivores and so on.*

48. Why is the chain a circle? *Because it keeps repeating itself over and over again as animals and plants grow, reproduce, and die.*

CENTRAL IDEA: A food chain is a circle of life that never ends.

What Eats What in a Rain Forest Food Chain:
THOUGHT CAPTURER

Starting with the cacao leaf, fill in the circles with the names of animals or plants that come before each other in the food chain. Then use the line of the outside circle to write a sentence that describes what is happening in the diagram.

Name: _____

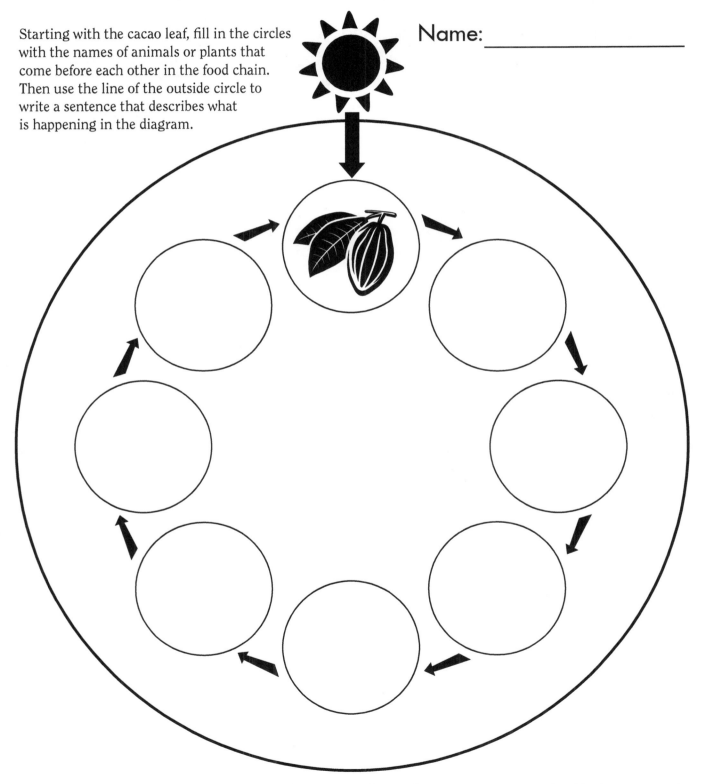

©2015 Linda Feaman and Nancy Geldermann from *Unlocking Close Reading*. This page may be reproduced for classroom use only.

Why is the food chain like a circle? How do you know?

_____

_____

_____

_____

What Eats What in a Rain Forest Food Chain:
THOUGHT CAPTURER ANSWER KEY

Recommended for Grade 2

Starting with the cacao leaf, fill in the circles with the names of animals or plants that come before each other in the food chain. Then use the line of the outside circle to write a sentence that describes what is happening in the diagram.

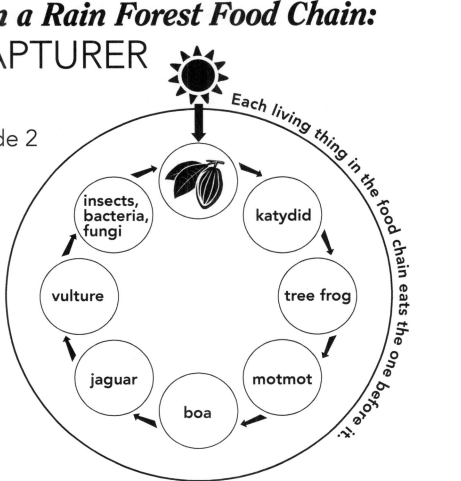

Each living thing in the food chain eats the one before it.

- insects, bacteria, fungi
- katydid
- tree frog
- motmot
- boa
- jaguar
- vulture

Why is the food chain like a circle? How do you know?

The food chain is like a circle because it doesn't have a beginning or an end. The plants and animals in the food chain provide food for each other, but all of the food energy eventually returns to the soil to help more plants grow. This makes the food chain never-ending, like a circle.

What Eats What in a Rain Forest Food Chain:
THOUGHT CAPTURER

Name one living thing from the text that fits each category.

Name: _____

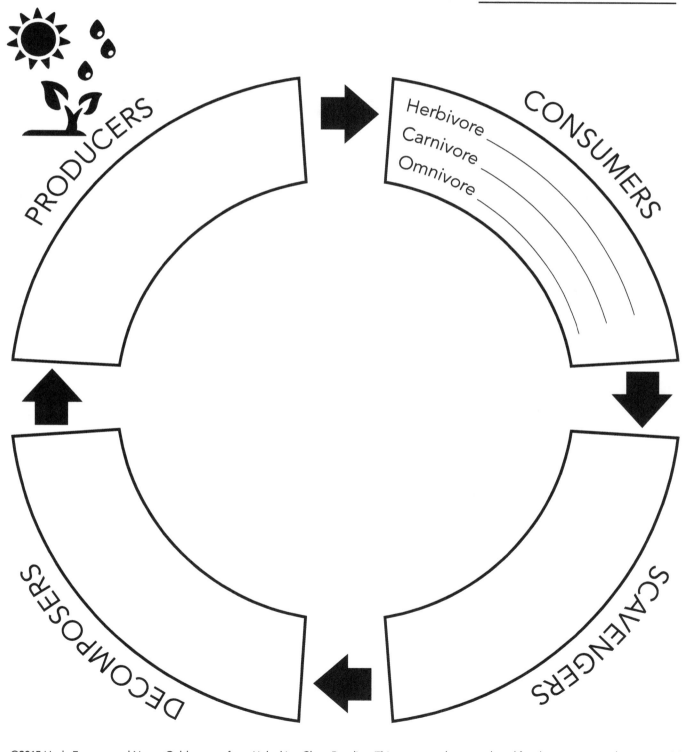

PRODUCERS

CONSUMERS

Herbivore

Carnivore _____

Omnivore _____

SCAVENGERS

DECOMPOSERS

Why is the food chain never-ending?

_____

_____

_____

_____

What Eats What in a Rain Forest Food Chain:
THOUGHT CAPTURER ANSWER KEY

Recommended
for Grade 3

Name one living thing from the
text that fits each category.

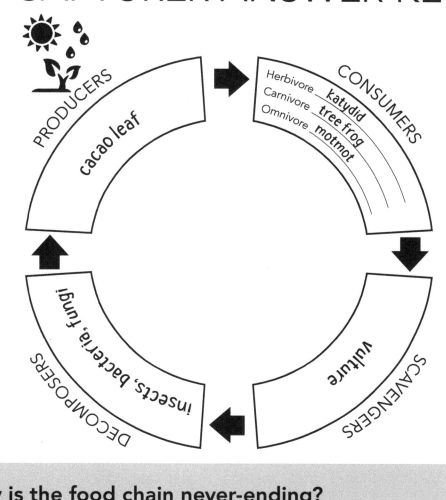

PRODUCERS
cacao leaf

CONSUMERS
Herbivore — katydid
Carnivore — tree frog
Omnivore — motmot

SCAVENGERS
vulture

DECOMPOSERS
insects, bacteria, fungi

Why is the food chain never-ending?

The food chain is never-ending because it is a circle of life. Each animal or

plant in the circle gets its food energy from the "one before it." The chain

never ends because when the jaguar dies, a scavenger eats it. Decomposers

break down the dead jaguar and nutrients from the jaguar's body return to

the soil. The nutrients from the dead jaguar provide food energy for a new

cacao tree to grow, and the cycle of life will start all over again.

What If There Were No Sea Otters?

by Suzanne Slade

1 Sea otters know how to have fun. Found in the northern Pacific Ocean, these furry mammals love to tumble and twirl in the water. Sea otters live in kelp forests near the shore, along with colorful fish, crabs, clams, and sea urchins.

2 All living things in the ocean ecosystem depend on each other for food. Plants and animals are connected to one another in a food chain. There are lots of different food chains in the ocean ecosystem. The sea otter belongs to more than one. When many food chains connect, they make a food web.

3 Sea otters are big eaters. One adult otter can munch as much as 25 pounds of food a day. Sea otters enjoy all sorts of tasty treats, including fish, snails, and mussels. But a sea otter's favorite meal is sea urchins.

4 Sharks and killer whales hunt sea otters, but people are the biggest danger. Sea otters get tangled in fishing nets. They're hit by speeding boats. Litter and oil spills turn the animals' water homes into garbage dumps. As a result, sea otters have already disappeared from some areas. And those areas have changed—for the worse.

> *What If There Were No Sea Otters?*

 5

Sometimes a plant or animal species is so important that without it, many other species could become extinct. It's called a keystone species. Sea otters are a keystone species. Keystone species help make sure an ecosystem has many types of life in it.

 6

What would happen if sea otters became extinct? Without hungry otters to dine on them, sea urchin populations would start to grow out of control.

 7

Tasty kelp leaves and algae make the perfect meal for sea urchins. But the sea urchins would eat faster than plants could grow. Soon sea urchins would gobble up nearly all plant life near the shore.

 8

Sea urchins aren't the only ocean animals that eat plants. Fish, crabs, and snails do too. But before long, they would be in danger. They wouldn't be able to find enough food.

 9

And plants aren't just food. Kelp forests make great hideouts. Small animals hide in the kelp to escape big animals that may eat them. Some fish lay eggs in the kelp and raise their young there. Others use groups of plants as markers to find their way. Without plants, many fish and other small sea animals wouldn't survive.

10

Octopuses and sharks don't eat plants, but they eat fish and crabs. And fish and crabs rely on plants for survival. If plants disappear, so do large sea animals.

11

If sea otters are killed or become extinct, what was once a place filled with many kinds of life would now look very different. No sea otters would be gliding through leafy kelp forests. No clusters of clams would be lying on the ocean floor. No crabs would be clicking their claws. No graceful, colorful fish would be swimming by. What there would be are lots of sea stars and hungry sea urchins.

12

Ocean ecosystems where sea otters have disappeared are called urchin barrens. Barrens are overcrowded with sea urchins and sea stars and have little plant life.

13

So what would happen if sea otters became extinct? A LOT!

14

One small change, such as the loss of sea otters, can make a big difference in the lives of countless plants and animals. That's why it's so important to take care of our ocean ecosystems.

15

It's critical! More sea otters mean stronger food chains in our oceans. Hunting sea otters is against the law in most places. Special laws also help reduce pollution in our oceans. Wildlife teams are reintroducing sea otters to areas where they once lived. These otter families are doing well and having new pups. Thanks to caring people around the world, more than 90,000 sea otters now splash in the northern Pacific where there were once less than half that many.

Note: It is recommended that charts of both a food chain and a food web are posted and explained before reading so students understand the interdependency concepts presented in the text. Use the animal examples in the text for the food chain and food web examples.

What If There Were No Sea Otters?:
TEACHER DISCUSSION GUIDE
Grade Level: 2–4, Guided Reading Level: N, Lexile Level: 820L

1

Sea otters know how to have fun. Found in **A**the northern Pacific Ocean, these furry mammals love to tumble and twirl in the water. Sea otters live in **B**kelp forests near the shore, **C**along with colorful fish, crabs, clams, and sea urchins.

2

All living things in the ocean **D**ecosystem **E**depend on each other for food. Plants and animals are connected to one another in a **F**food chain. There are lots of different food chains in the ocean ecosystem. The sea otter belongs to more than one. When many food chains connect, they make a **G**food web.

3

Sea otters are **H**big eaters. One adult otter can munch as much as 25 pounds of food a day. Sea otters enjoy all sorts of tasty treats, including fish, snails, and mussels. But a sea otter's **I**favorite meal is sea urchins.

A 1. What part of the world do sea otters live in? *The northern Pacific Ocean*

B 2. Where in the ocean do they live? *In kelp forests near the shore*

C 3. What lives with them? *Fish, crabs, clams, and sea urchins*

D 4. What is an *ecosystem*? *Elicit or define: it is made up of all the plants, animals, and nonliving things (soil, water, sunlight, etc.) in an area that depend on each other to live. In a working ecosystem, there is a natural balance among predator, prey, and nonliving things.*

E 5. What does *depend* mean? *Elicit from context: to rely on or count on someone or something.*

6. How do the living things in an ecosystem get food from each other? *They eat other plants and animals in their food chains.*

7. How are animals connected to one another in a food chain? *They are connected because they depend on each other for food.*

F 8. What is a *food chain?* Refer to the charts from lesson's Note: *A sequence of what eats what in an ecosystem. The chain starts with an energy source (usually the sun) and ends with the top predator (an animal with few or no enemies).*

G 9. What is the difference between a food chain and a food web? *A food web is made up of several interconnected food chains in which animals may eat more than one thing.*

10. Are sea otters part of a food web? *Yes, because they belong to more than one food chain.*

H 11. What makes sea otters big eaters? *They eat as much as 25 pounds of food a day.*

12. What do they eat? *Fish, snails, mussels, and sea urchins*

I 13. What is their favorite food? *Sea urchins*

4

J Sharks and killer whales hunt sea otters, but people are the biggest danger. **K** Sea otters get tangled in fishing nets. They're hit by speeding boats. Litter and oil spills turn the animals' water homes into garbage dumps. **L** As a result, sea otters have already disappeared from some areas. And those areas have **M** changed–for the worse.

5

Sometimes a plant or animal species is so important that without it, many other species could become extinct. It's called a **N** keystone species. Sea otters are a keystone species. Keystone species help make sure an ecosystem has many types of life in it.

6

What would happen if sea otters became **O** extinct? Without hungry otters to **P** dine on them, sea urchin **Q** populations would start to **R** grow out of control.

7

Tasty kelp leaves and algae make the **S** perfect meal for sea urchins. **T** But the sea urchins would eat faster than plants could grow. **U** Soon sea urchins would gobble up nearly all plant life near the shore.

J 14. Which animals eat sea otters? *Sharks and killer whales*

15. What is the biggest threat to sea otters? *People*

K 16. What do people do that threatens sea otters? *They catch them in fishing nets; hit sea otters with speedboats; and cause water pollution (especially oil spills), which poisons the water in the ecosystem.*

L 17. What happens as a result of the human threats? *Sea otters die and disappear from the ecosystem.*

M 18. What is the author saying here? *When the sea otters disappear from the ecosystem, the area changes in a bad way.*

N 19. What is a *keystone species? Have students turn and talk to identify context clues to define, then share out. A keystone species is one that plays a "key" role in the survival of the ecosystem. It keeps the balance of predators and prey and without it, other animals and plants in the system could die and/or become extinct.*

O 20. Refer to the question in the title to elicit a definition for extinct. *No longer in existence*

21. *At this point, introduce the Chain Reaction Chart (page 71) to help students visualize and record the answer to the question posed in the title as well as in paragraph 6.*

P 22. What does it mean to dine on something? *It is a synonym for eat, but it also means to eat the main meal of the day. The sea otters' main meal (favorite) is sea urchins. Elicit or discuss with students that it can be inferred that because sea otters eat so much each day, they eat a lot of sea urchins.*

Q 23. What is a *population? Elicit or define: the number of animals or plants of a specific species in an ecosystem.*

R 24. What does it mean to *grow out of control? To grow so fast and so much that it becomes unmanageable; the ecosystem would become unbalanced because there would be far too many sea urchins.*

S 25. What do sea urchins like to eat? *Kelp leaves and algae*

T 26. Why would this happen? *The increase in the sea urchin population would cause the plants to be eaten in a greater number. Note: Be sure students understand that this is the next step in the chain reaction and that it is a direct result of the sea otters not eating the sea urchins.*

U 27. What is the result of the plant life being eaten faster than it can grow? *The plant life near the shore will disappear.*

8

Sea urchins aren't the only ocean animals that eat plants. Fish, crabs, and snails do too. But before long, **V** they would be in danger. They wouldn't be able to find enough food.

9

And plants aren't just **W** food. Kelp forests make great hideouts. Small animals hide in the kelp to escape big animals that may eat them. Some fish lay eggs in the kelp and raise their young there. Others use groups of plants as **X** markers to find their way. **Y** Without plants, many fish and other small sea animals wouldn't survive.

10

Octopuses and sharks don't eat plants, but they eat fish and crabs. And fish and crabs rely on plants for survival. **Z** If plants disappear, so do large sea animals.

11

If sea otters are killed or become extinct, what was once a place filled with many kinds of life **AA** would now look very different. No sea otters would be gliding through leafy kelp forests. No clusters of clams would be lying on the ocean floor. No crabs would be clicking their claws. **BB** No graceful, colorful fish would be swimming by. **CC** What there would be are lots of sea stars and hungry sea urchins.

12

Ocean ecosystems where sea otters have disappeared are called urchin barrens. Barrens are overcrowded with sea urchins and sea stars and **DD** have little plant life.

V 28. Why would fish, crabs, and snails be in danger if the plant life disappeared? *Turn and talk, then share out. Be sure students understand the interdependency of the animals and plants within the ecosystem.*

W 29. What else do plants provide besides food? *Safety for animals to hide out and lay eggs*

X 30. What is a *marker*? *Elicit from context: something that is used to mark a route to help animals find their way in the ocean.*

Y 31. Besides not having plants to eat, why wouldn't some fish and other sea animals survive without plants? *They need them for protection and direction. They might be eaten, their offspring wouldn't survive, or they could be lost and unable to find their way to another safe place.*

Z 32. Why would large sea animals disappear if plants disappeared? *If the fish and small animals that the octopuses and sharks eat disappear because there are no plants for them to eat, the large sea animals wouldn't be able to find food and they would go elsewhere or die.*

AA 33. Why would the ecosystem look very different if the sea otters were gone? *Turn and talk, then share out. Elicit that the absence of sea otters affect the populations of all of the other animals and plants in the ecosystem. That is why it is a keystone species; all other organisms in the ecosystem depend on sea otters to balance the populations.*

BB 34. Why does the author repeat the word *no* in every sentence? *To emphasize the impact the absence of sea otters would have on the ecosystems. There would be no other animals because without the keystone species, the ecosystem falls apart.*

CC 35. Why would there be lots of sea urchins, and why would they be hungry? *There would be a lot of sea urchins because they are the favorite prey of the sea otter. They would "grow out of control" without the sea otters to eat many of them each day. They would be hungry because they would eat up all the plants before they could grow back.*

DD 36. *Finish the Chain Reaction Chart at this point, return to the last sentence in paragraph 5, and ask students to turn and talk to explain what the statement means. They should be able to explain the balance created and maintained by the keystone species, and how that balance includes many different kinds of animals because the food web is dependent on it.*

13

So what would happen if sea otters became extinct? **EE**A LOT!

14

One small change, such as the loss of sea otters, can make a big difference in the lives of countless plants and animals. **FF**That's why it's so important to take care of our ocean ecosystems.

15

It's **GG**critical! **HH**More sea otters mean stronger food chains in our oceans. Hunting sea otters is against the law in most places. Special laws also help reduce pollution in our oceans. Wildlife teams are reintroducing sea otters to areas where they once lived. These otter families are doing well and having new pups. **II**Thanks to caring people around the world, more than 90,000 sea otters now splash in the northern Pacific where there were once less than half that many.

EE 37. *Refer to share out after question 36, and ask students to reiterate if they need to.*

FF 38. Why is it so important for us to take care of something that is part of nature? *Because the ocean ecosystems would be fine if it weren't for people causing it to be in danger.*

GG 39. What does *critical* mean? *Elicit or define: having the potential to become disastrous; at a point of crisis.*

HH 40. Why is this important? *Stronger food chains mean more balanced ocean ecosystems and a decreased threat of animals becoming endangered or extinct.*

II 41. What steps are we taking to re-establish the ocean ecosystems that have been lost and to maintain the ones in existence? *Accept reasonable answers based on text evidence.*

CENTRAL IDEA: Sea otters are keystone species that need to be protected from human dangers in order to maintain balance in the ocean ecosystem.

What If There Were No Sea Otters?: CHAIN REACTION CHART

Name: _____

CAUSE	EFFECT

⬇

Sometimes a plant or animal species is so important that without it many other species would become extinct. It is called a **keystone species**.

What If There Were No Sea Otters?:
CHAIN REACTION CHART ANSWER KEY

CAUSE	EFFECT
Sea otters disappear	Sea urchins grow out of control (too many)

CAUSE	EFFECT
Abundance of sea urchins eat kelp faster than it can grow	Plants near shore disappear

CAUSE	EFFECT
Plants disappear from ecosystem	Fish, crabs, snails are in danger because they also eat plants and can't find food Fish and small animals use plants for protection, to lay eggs, and for markers to find their way

CAUSE	EFFECT
Fish, crabs, snails die	Large sea predators (octopuses and sharks) have no food

CAUSE	EFFECT
Large predators die or go elsewhere	Sea urchins keep multiplying and create an urchin barren

CAUSE	EFFECT
No sea otters No fish No crabs No snails	Lots of hungry sea urchins (What do they eat?)

Sometimes a plant or animal species is so important that without it many other species would become extinct. It is called a **keystone species**.

Note: This chart should be used as a prewriting organizer for the constructed response. (See following page.)

What If There Were No Sea Otters?: ANNOTATED CONSTRUCTED RESPONSE EXEMPLARS

Prompt: What does the author **really** want us to know about sea otters and the ocean's ecosystem?

Grade 2

Transitioning second graders to the constructed response format expected in grades 3 and 4 requires that they understand its basic components. For this lesson, students are provided with the first three parts of the constructed response (answer/central idea and two pieces of text evidence with rationale) and then asked to respond to questions to elicit the two-part conclusion (Part A: synthesis and Part B: a new idea).

Introduce the following elements of a constructed response by posting or by providing student copies of items 1–3 below for the whole class. Remind students of the prompt: What does the author **really** want us to know about sea otters and the ocean ecosystem?

1. Answer/Central Idea: *The author wants us to know that certain animals, like the sea otter, are very important to the ocean's ecosystem, and we must protect them to be sure that all animals can survive.*

2. Text Evidence #1 with Rationale: *"All living things in the ocean ecosystem depend on each other for food. Plants and animals are connected to one another in a food chain." When a food chain is balanced, all of the animals have plenty of food. If it becomes unbalanced because plants or animals disappear, all of the animals and plants in the food chain are affected.*

3. Text Evidence #2 with Rationale: *"Sometimes a plant or animal species is so important that without it, many other species could become extinct." The sea otter is a keystone species. That means many animals depend on it to maintain balance in the ecosystem. Without sea otters, sea urchins grow out of control. That starts a chain reaction that threatens the lives of all the other plants and animals in the ecosystem.*

After providing the previous information, ask students to complete the constructed response by answering questions 4 and 5 below. Have them use the Chain Reaction Chart for reference.

4. What will happen if sea otters become extinct? *The sea otter is an important part of the ocean ecosystem because it is a keystone species. If sea otters become extinct, many other species in the ecosystem will become extinct too.*

5. What new idea does this give you? *People need to protect sea otters so they can do their job to help keep the ocean a safe place for all animals.*

Note: The following annotated exemplars are aligned with the Constructed Response Instructional Rubric Grades 3–4 (pages 155–156) and the Constructed Response Student Checklist Grades 3–4 (page 157).

Grade 3

A Answer/Central Idea

B Text Evidence #1 with Rationale

C Text Evidence #2 with Rationale

D Text Evidence #3 with Rationale

E Conclusion Part A

F Conclusion Part B

The author wants us to know that sea otters are really important for keeping the ocean healthy, and that we have to help keep them alive so other animals can survive **A** too. "Plants and animals are connected to one another in a food chain." Sea otters eat sea urchins, and sea urchins eat plants that other animals need to eat too. If one part of the chain is broken because an animal becomes extinct, the other parts will be broken **B** also. "Sometimes a plant or animal species is so important that without it, many other species could become extinct." Sea otters are called a keystone species because other animals depend on them for their own survival. For example, sea otters really like to eat sea urchins. If the sea otters were gone, there would be too many sea urchins. They would eat too many plants and not leave enough food for fish and other ocean animals. This would make some animals become extinct because their food would be eaten up by the **C** sea urchins. The author also wants us to remember that sometimes humans are the ones who cause animals like the sea otter to disappear. "People are the biggest danger. Sea otters get tangled in fishing nets. They're hit by speeding boats. Litter and oil spills turn the animals' water homes into garbage dumps." All of these things people do have caused otters to lose their **D** homes. In places the otters have left, the sea urchins have grown out of control and "those areas have changed—for the worse." The author wants us to know that we need to protect animals like the sea otter and make sure they don't lose their places to live. We need to bring in new sea otters to be sure the ecosystem stays **E** strong. Humans need to make sure we help keep the ocean's ecosystem healthy. Many different plants and animals need keystone species like the sea otter to help them stay alive. Sea otters have an important job to do, and we need to help them do **F** it.

Grade 4

The author wants us to know that without sea otters, the ocean ecosystem can't work like it is supposed to, and we need to help make sure that it **G** does. If sea otters disappear, the ocean ecosystem can't work right. When sea otters aren't around to gobble up sea urchins, the urchin populations start to "grow out of control." Urchins eat too much kelp and take food away from other animals, and before you know it, some kinds of animals are out of food. "Sea otters have already disappeared from some areas. And those areas have changed—for the **H** worse." Sea otters are called a keystone species. This means they "help make sure an ecosystem has many types of life in it." This is important because without sea otters, "many other species could become extinct." Keystone species are "key" to the survival of the plants and animals that live in the same area. Without them, plants and animals will die. It will become a place with only one type of animal, like a sea urchin **I** barren. The author points out that the main reason sea otters disappear is because of humans. We need to protect sea otters from "fishing nets" and from "speeding boats" and from "litter and oil spills" that can kill them. We need to try and raise new sea otter families in places where they've disappeared. We also need to help rebuild food webs by "reintroducing sea otters to areas where they once lived." "One small change, such as the loss of sea otters, can make a big difference in the lives of countless plants and **J** animals." It's not just food that animals need to stay alive. They also need a healthy place to live. If the sea otters leave and the sea urchins eat up all the plants, other animals won't have a place to hide or lay their eggs. They might not even be able to find their way around. Without keystone species like the sea otter, all of the animals are affected in all kinds of **K** ways. The author wants us to know how important sea otters are to ocean ecosystems. Because we are responsible for many of the sea otters disappearing, we should start being more responsible for their **L** protection.

G Answer/Central Idea

H Text Evidence #1 with Rationale

I Text Evidence #2 with Rationale

J Text Evidence #3 with Rationale

K Conclusion Part A

L Conclusion Part B

Albert Einstein
by Dana Meachen Rau

1

Have you ever wondered how the world works? A scientist named Albert Einstein always wondered about that. He thought the world was an amazing place. He was interested in the huge objects found in outer space as well as the tiny bits of matter that can be seen only through a microscope. He had many new ideas, or theories, about the way the world works. He looked at the world in a way no one else ever had.

2

Albert's sense of wonder began when he was a young boy. He liked quiet games that needed a lot of thought, such as building with blocks or making houses of cards.

3

When Albert was 5 years old, his father showed him a compass. A compass is an instrument with a needle that shows the four directions—north, south, east, and west. People use it to show them which way they are going. Einstein was fascinated by the way the compass moved. The needle always pointed north no matter how he turned the compass. It made him think the world does not always work the way we expect it to.

4

His parents sent Albert and his younger sister, Maja, to a German school. Albert did not like school, though. He thought the teachers were too strict. They always wanted the children to remember a lot of facts. Albert had trouble memorizing words. He felt more comfortable with numbers and ideas. He once said, "Imagination is more important than knowledge."

5

He did not do well on tests, either. He got good grades only in his favorite subjects—math and science. Albert knew so much about these subjects that sometimes his teachers did not know the answers to his questions. He studied math and science outside of school too. His favorite book to read at home was a math book given to him when he was 12.

6

Albert left school when he was only 15 because he disliked it so much. He later earned a diploma from a school in Switzerland. He liked this school a lot and got good grades there. His grades were good enough to continue studying at a university. In 1896, Albert began to study physics at a university in Zurich, Switzerland. Just as in grade school, Albert never liked going to classes or taking tests. He still worked hard, though. He graduated four years later.

7

Einstein wanted to be a professor, but he could not find work. So he took an office job in 1902. He had a lot of extra time to study physics on his own.

8

In 1905, Einstein wrote many papers about his theories of how the world works. His most famous paper changed science forever. He introduced the theory of relativity.

9

Since the 1600s, people had believed in the ideas of a scientist named Sir Isaac Newton. Newton said that space and time never change. He said nature had certain laws that are never broken. People were used to this view of the world.

10

Einstein had a completely different idea. He believed that space and time do change. He studied energy and the speed of light. He found that objects change depending on how fast they are moving.

11

Einstein's ideas made him famous. He became a professor of physics in the European cities of Zurich and Prague. In 1914, he moved to Germany to become a professor at the University of Berlin. He continued his research there but did not teach classes. In 1921, Einstein was given a special award—the Nobel Prize in Physics. Now people all over the world knew about Einstein and his ideas. They wrote articles about him and took photos of him for many newspapers.

12

Even when he became famous, though, Einstein was still a simple man. He said, "A table, a chair, a bowl of fruit and a violin; what else does a man need to be happy?" Einstein cared deeply for the world he wondered about so much. He wanted everyone in the world to live in peace.

13

All his life, Einstein was fascinated by the way the world worked. He used his imagination to form his scientific ideas. And he wished that the world would be a peaceful place. He once said, "Only a life lived for others is a life worthwhile."

14

Some people have called Einstein the most important person of the twentieth century. He changed the world with his ideas. He taught people how to wonder.

Albert Einstein:
TEACHER DISCUSSION GUIDE

Grade Level: 2–4, Guided Reading Level: P

1

Have you ever **ⓐ**wondered how the world works? A scientist named Albert Einstein always **ⓑ**wondered about that. He thought the world was an amazing place. He was interested in **ⓒ**the huge objects found in outer space as well as **ⓓ**the tiny bits of matter that can be seen only through a microscope. He had many new ideas, or **ⓔ**theories, **ⓕ**about the way the world works. He looked at the world **ⓖ**in a way no one else ever had.

2

Albert's **ⓗ**sense of wonder began when he was a young boy. He liked quiet games that needed a lot of thought, such as **ⓘ**building with blocks or making houses of cards.

ⓐ 1. What does *wonder* mean in this context? *To be curious about, to want to know more about*

ⓑ 2. What did Albert Einstein always wonder about? *How the world works*

ⓒ 3. What are some huge objects found in outer space? *The sun, the moon*

ⓓ 4. What is a microscope, and what kind of things can be seen through one? *Elicit or explain: a device used to view objects too small to be seen closely just using the eye.*

ⓔ 5. What are *theories? New ideas*

ⓕ 6. What did Albert Einstein have many theories, or new ideas, about? *How the world works, from outer space to tiny bits of matter and everything in between*

ⓖ 7. What does it mean to look at the world in a way no one else does? *To have a different perspective or point of view than others do*

8. How did Albert Einstein develop his different perspective? *By wondering about the way the world works*

ⓗ 9. What is a *sense of wonder? Elicit or explain: asking questions that focus on the uniqueness of the world around us.*

10. Why is this important? *His curiosity began when he was little, which indicates his mind was extraordinary from a very young age.*

ⓘ 11. What kind of thinking is needed for these games? *Elicit or discuss strategic thinking, such as: problem solving, creating balance and support, designing, predicting, trial and error.*

12. How is that kind of thinking different from the thinking in other childhood games? *The type of games Einstein liked required complex thinking, and most children's games require basic, simpler thinking skills.*

3

When Albert was 5 years old, his father showed him a compass. **J**A compass is an instrument with a needle that shows the four directions–north, south, east, and west. People use it to show them which way they are going. Einstein was fascinated by the way the compass moved. **K**The needle always pointed north no matter how he turned the compass. It made him think **L**the world does not always work the way we expect it to.

4

His parents sent Albert and his younger sister, Maja, to a German school. Albert did not like school, though. He thought the teachers were too strict. They always wanted the children to remember a lot of facts. Albert had trouble memorizing words. He **M**felt more comfortable with numbers and ideas. He once said, **N**"Imagination is more important than knowledge."

5

He did not do well on tests, either. **O**He got good grades only in his favorite subjects—math and science. Albert knew so much about these subjects that **P**sometimes his teachers did not know the answers to his questions. He studied math and science outside of school too. His favorite book to read at home was a math book **Q**given to him when he was 12.

J 13. If Albert's father told him that people use a compass to show them which way they are going, and he showed him a compass that had a moving needle and all four directions on it, what was Albert expecting the needle to do when he held the compass? *He was expecting the needle to point in the direction he was going.*

K 14. What did the needle do that was different from what he expected? *It always pointed north instead of in the direction he was going.*

15. Why did the compass movement fascinate him? *No matter what he did, the needle always pointed north. It made him wonder why.*

L 16. How old was Albert when he was thinking this way? *5*

17. What does that tell you about his mind? *That it was unique*

18. How might this realization have led him to "look at the world in a way no one else ever had"? *By expecting the unexpected, his mind was open to new ideas about the way the world worked.*

M 19. Why would he feel more comfortable with numbers and ideas than memorizing facts? *Einstein's mind was full of questions and new ideas that took a lot of thinking to develop. Memorization is not thoughtful, and he preferred to think.*

N 20. What does *imagination* mean in this sentence? *Elicit from context clues or define: the ability of the mind to be creative or resourceful; inventiveness, innovation.*

21. How does this statement explain why he was more comfortable with numbers and ideas? *Memorizing facts on their own isn't as meaningful as applying facts to thinking. He thought that using facts to create something new or to find a solution to a problem was more valuable than just knowing the facts.*

O 22. Why does this make sense? *He was so curious about the world that he didn't pay attention to the things he didn't wonder about.*

P 23. What does this tell you about Einstein? *His sense of wonder helped him learn a lot more than even his teachers knew.*

Q 24. What does this say about him? *Turn and talk. Elicit that most 12-year-olds don't read a math book for fun and that he was exceptional at a very young age.*

6

Albert left school when he was only 15 because **R**he disliked it so much. He later earned a diploma from **S**a school in Switzerland. He liked this school a lot and got good grades there. His grades were good enough to continue studying at a university. In 1896, Albert began to study physics at a university in Zurich, Switzerland. Just as in grade school, **T**Albert never liked going to classes or taking tests. He still worked hard, though. He graduated four years later.

7

Einstein wanted to be a professor, but he could not find work. So he took an office job in 1902. **U**He had a lot of extra time to study physics on his own.

8

In 1905, Einstein wrote many papers about his **V**theories of how the world works. **W**His most famous paper changed science forever. He **X**introduced the **Y**theory of relativity.

9

ZSince the 1600s, people had believed in the ideas of a scientist named Sir Isaac Newton. Newton said that space and time never change. He said nature had certain laws that are never broken. People were used to this view of the world.

10

AAEinstein had a completely different idea. He believed that space and time do change. He studied energy and the speed of light. He found that objects change depending on how fast they are moving.

R 25. Why did Einstein dislike school so much? *Turn and talk. Accept reasonable answers based on the text, including: He was so bright and curious and school was limiting to him.*

S 26. What had to be different about this school? *It must have let him be more imaginative and allowed him to broaden his sense of wonder.*

T 27. What does this tell you about him? *He knew the value of learning despite the fact that he didn't like school; he was persistent, determined.*

U 28. What is *physics*? *Elicit or define: the study of matter and energy and how they interact with each other; physics uses the scientific method to formulate and test hypotheses that are based on observations of the natural world. Note: Make connections between physics and Einstein's wonder about "how the world works."*

29. Why would he continue to study physics on his own? *His sense of wonder never left him, he was still curious about how the world worked.*

V 30. How did he develop his new ideas about how the world works? *When he studied physics on his own, he experimented with new ideas that came from his wondering about the world and how it works. Eventually, the experiments led him to discoveries about the physical world that no one else had ever made before.*

W 31. How could one person's idea change science forever? *Turn and talk. Elicit that his theory of relativity grew out of his unique sense of wonder. Einstein's ability to see things differently allowed him to open his mind to possibilities that others never could. He changed science forever because his theory of relativity allowed him to share his unique perspective with the world.*

X 32. What does *introduced* mean? *Elicit from context clues: to present for the first time.*

Y 33. *Note: Students do not need an explanation of the theory of relativity to understand its impact. Explain that Einstein used his unique way of looking at things to make an important scientific discovery.*

34. Why did his theory of relativity paper become so famous? *Because it changed the way people thought about how the world worked, and it taught other people the importance of wondering.*

Z 35. Why had people believed Newton's ideas for so long? *Because no one else had thought to "wonder" about them, so everyone believed they were true.*

36. What did Newton believe? *Space and time never change, certain laws of nature are never broken.*

AA 37. How did Einstein's ideas differ from Newton's? *Space and time* do *change, some laws of nature* can *be broken.*

11

Einstein's ideas made him famous. He became a professor of physics in the European cities of Zurich and Prague. In 1914, he moved to Germany to become a professor at the University of Berlin. **BB**He continued his research there but did not teach classes. In 1921, Einstein was given a **CC**special award—the Nobel Prize in Physics. **DD**Now people all over the world knew about Einstein and his ideas. They wrote articles about him and took photos of him for many newspapers.

12

Even when he became famous, though, Einstein was still a **EE**simple man. He said, "A table, a chair, a bowl of fruit and a violin; what else does a man need to be happy?" **FF**Einstein cared deeply for the world he wondered about so much. He wanted everyone in the world to live in peace.

13

GGAll his life, Einstein was fascinated by the way the world worked. He used his imagination to form his scientific ideas. And he wished that the world would be a peaceful place. He once said, "Only a life lived for others is a life worthwhile."

14

Some people have called Einstein the most important person of the twentieth century. **HH**He changed the world with his ideas. He taught people how to wonder.

BB 38. What is *research? Elicit from context clues: investigation of a subject in order to answer questions or make discoveries about it.*

39. What *research* did Einstein continue? *Research in physics, his theory of relativity*

CC 40. What special award was Einstein given? *The Nobel Prize in Physics*

DD 41. How did people around the world find out about Einstein's ideas? *When he received the special award, it was announced to the whole world though newspaper articles from many different countries.*

EE 42. How could such a complex man be considered *simple? Despite his fame, he was happy with the basics of life: a place to rest, food to eat, and music.*

FF 43. Why did he care so deeply for the world he wondered about so much? *Turn and talk. Accept reasonable answers based on text evidence including: He spent his entire life wondering about how the world works that it makes sense he would want to take care of something he knew so much about.*

GG 44. How did Einstein turn his sense of wonder into his life's work? *His questioning showed him a new way of looking at things. His unique perspective led to new ideas, and the new ideas changed science forever.*

HH 45. How did he change the world by teaching people to wonder? *When people saw how Einstein's sense of wonder led to his amazing discoveries, they too started to look at the world differently. Thinking with wonder has become the way of the world thanks to Einstein and his gift of wonder.*

CENTRAL IDEA: A young boy with a sense of wonder grew up to be a creative genius who changed science forever.

Albert Einstein:
READER RESPONSE

Name: _____

Albert Einstein was a creative genius whose endless curiosity and sense of wonder changed science forever.

Answer these questions about Albert Einstein.

1 He wondered about how the world works and "looked at the world in a way no one else ever had."

What does this sentence make you think?

_____

_____

_____

2 Instead of accepting current scientific ideas, Einstein was open to new possibilities. He soon began to write about his own theories of "how the world works."

What do these sentences make you think?

_____

_____

_____

3 Einstein "used his imagination to form his scientific ideas."

What does this sentence make you think?

_____

_____

_____

Einstein taught people to think differently. "He taught people how to wonder."

Albert Einstein: READER RESPONSE ANSWER KEY

Recommended for Grade 2

Note: This scaffolded constructed response format is intended to introduce students to the kind of thinking and writing structure required for the constructed response paragraphs expected for grades 3 and 4. It parallels the format of the Thought Capturer (see page 150) as well as the Constructed Response Instructional Rubric Grades 3–4. (See pages 155–156.)

Albert Einstein was a creative genius whose endless curiosity and sense of wonder changed science forever.

Answer these questions about Albert Einstein.

1 He wondered about how the world works and "looked at the world in a way no one else ever had."

What does this sentence make you think?

He was curious, and it made him think about how things work.

2 Instead of accepting current scientific ideas, Einstein was open to new possibilities. He soon began to write about his own theories of "how the world works."

What do these sentences make you think?

He didn't just follow what other scientists said.

He made up new ideas of his own.

3 Einstein "used his imagination to form his scientific ideas."

What does this sentence make you think?

Einstein's imagination helped him think about how things in science

might be different.

Einstein taught people to think differently. "He taught people how to wonder."

Albert Einstein:
ANNOTATED CONSTRUCTED RESPONSE EXEMPLARS

Recommended for Grades 3–4

Prompt: What does the author **really** want us to know about Albert Einstein?

Note: Annotated exemplars are aligned with the Constructed Response Instructional Rubric Grades 3–4 (pages 155–156) and the Constructed Response Student Checklist Grades 3–4 (page 157).

Grade 3

Ⓐ Answer/Central Idea

Ⓑ Text Evidence #1 with Rationale

Ⓒ Text Evidence #2 with Rationale

Ⓓ Text Evidence #3 with Rationale

Ⓔ Conclusion Part A

Ⓕ Conclusion Part B

Albert Einstein was a very smart man who asked questions about the world and changed science with the new ideas he **Ⓐ**discovered. He wondered about how the world works and "looked at the world in a way no one else ever had." When he was just 5, his father gave him a compass. It worked differently than he thought it would and it made him wonder why. This was the beginning of his wondering about things and how they worked. He was different than other **Ⓑ**kids. When he grew up he still wondered about things and didn't think like other scientists. After college he looked at the ideas of another scientist named Sir Isaac Newton. He thought about what Newton said about physics and thought maybe he was wrong. Newton said that time and space never change but Einstein did his own research and found a different answer. He found out that "objects change depending on how fast they are moving." He came up with his own new ideas that changed science **Ⓒ**forever. These new ideas made him famous. He even got the Nobel Prize in Physics. He used his imagination to think of new ideas and he didn't just follow what other people **Ⓓ**thought. The author wants us to understand that Einstein wasn't just a scientist. He was very **Ⓔ**smart. He made other people want to learn new things too. He changed how they looked at the world. He taught people to question and wonder about things around **Ⓕ**them.

Grade 4

Albert Einstein was a creative genius whose never-ending curiosity and sense of wonder changed science **(G)** forever. He wondered about how the world works and "looked at the world in a way no one else ever had." When he was only 5, his father showed him a compass and he wondered why it worked the way it did. He played with the compass and it "made him think the world does not always work the way we expect it to." Einstein's curiosity made him different than other kids and made him think and wonder about how things might really **(H)** work. Instead of just following other scientists' ideas, Einstein had creative new ideas. After finishing his college studies, Einstein studied physics on his own. He soon began to write about his own "theories of how the world works." This area of science had been studied by a scientist named Sir Isaac Newton. "Newton said that space and time never change. He said nature had certain laws that are never broken. People were used to this view of the world." Because of his sense of wonder, Einstein did his own research of energy and the speed of light. "He found that objects change depending on how fast they are moving." His curiosity made him question the usual way of thinking and come up with new ideas of his **(I)** own. Einstein introduced the theory of relativity because of his studies. His research and new ideas about how the world works made him famous all around the world. He was even given the Nobel Prize in Physics. Einstein "used his imagination to form his scientific ideas." The ability to wonder made him think about new ideas and even change science **(J)** forever. The author wants us to understand that Einstein wasn't just a scientist. He was a creative genius. He had a way of looking at the world differently than everybody else and because he cared so much about it, he taught others to look at the world differently **(K)** too. He taught people to think differently. "He taught people how to **(L)** wonder."

(G) Answer/Central Idea

(H) Text Evidence #1 with Rationale

(I) Text Evidence #2 with Rationale

(J) Text Evidence #3 with Rationale

(K) Conclusion Part A

(L) Conclusion Part B

Humpback Whales

by Anna Claybourne

1

Humpback whales are very big, powerful whales. They are among the biggest of all sea creatures and have enormous flippers and tails. They are also known for their amazing singing and their long-distance travels, or migrations.

2

A humpback whale is up to 60 feet long and can weigh over 30 tons—as much as one thousand 10-year-old children! Most humpback whales are bluish-black on top, with a pale cream or white underside.

3

Humpbacks do not really have humps, but rather slightly humped dorsal fins. They get their name because when they dive, they curve their backs, making them look rounded, however, they do have lumps and bumps, called tubercles on their snout and flippers.

4

Intelligence is a hard thing to measure, especially in animals. However, whales and dolphins do seem to be very intelligent animals, along with chimps, orangutans, elephants, and crows. Humpback whales, like other whales, have been seen doing some very clever things.

5

Humpbacks seem to communicate with each other by making grunting and whistling sounds. These sounds are mostly made by mothers and calves calling to each other, but members of a pod also communicate with each other. Scientists do not yet know what all humpback sounds mean. But some calls do seem to have particular uses and meanings.

Compared to their body size, humpback brains are smaller than those of humans, chimps, or dolphins. But scientists have found that their brains show another sign of intelligence: they have a complex structure, or shape. The cortex, or outer part, of the humpback brain is deeply folded and made up of several layers, in a similar way to a human brain.

Scientists have found cells called spindle cells in humpbacks and other whales' brains. They are thought to be used in language and understanding emotions. The only other animals known to have them are humans, apes, chimpanzees, and elephants.

8

Learning is a sign of intelligence. Like humans, humpbacks learn a lot as they grow up, instead of behaving mainly according to instinct from birth. Adult humpbacks also learn things from each other, such as new songs and new methods of hunting.

9

Some humpback whales use "bubble-net" feeding in groups. One or more whales swim in circles, blowing streams of bubbles that rise toward the surface in a ring. Others herd shoals of fish into the "bubble-net" this creates. Then, the humpbacks swim up inside the "net" to feed. The fish are afraid to swim out through the bubbles.

Bubble-net hunting can even be seen as an example of using tools, another sign of high intelligence. Scientists think humpbacks' constantly changing songs show they have a culture, with shared social activities and creations. People who have encountered humpbacks often say the whales even seemed to want to communicate with them.

Does intelligence make an animal more "human"? Some people argue that chimps, whales, and other intelligent animals should not be hunted or harmed, since they are intelligent, like us. Should smart animals be treated better?

Humpback Whales:
TEACHER DISCUSSION GUIDE

Grade Level: 4–6, Guided Reading Level: P, Lexile Level: 1060L

1

ⒶHumpback whales are very big, powerful whales. They are among the biggest of all sea creatures and have enormous flippers and tails. They are also known for their amazing singing and their long-distance travels, or migrations.

2

A humpback whale is up to 60 feet long and can weigh over 30 tons—as much as one thousand 10-year-old children! Most humpback whales are bluish-black on top, with a pale cream or white underside.

3

Humpbacks do not really have humps, but rather slightly humped dorsal fins. **Ⓑ**They get their name because when they dive, they curve their backs, making them look rounded, however, they do have lumps and bumps, called tubercles on their snout and flippers.

4

ⒸIntelligence is a hard thing to measure, especially in animals. However, whales and dolphins do seem to be very intelligent animals, along with chimps, orangutans, elephants, and crows. Humpback whales, like other whales, have been seen doing some very clever things.

Ⓐ 1. Have students reread paragraphs 1–3. What are the major characteristics of humpback whales? *Turn and talk. Remind students to use specific details from the text.*

Ⓑ 2. Do humpback whales have humps on their backs? *No, they curve their backs when they dive, making them look rounded.*

3. What is the purpose of paragraphs 1–3? *They provide a description of the physical characteristics of humpback whales.*

Ⓒ 4. What is the topic of paragraph 4? *Some animals, including humpback whales, seem intelligent.*

5. Why did the author include the first three paragraphs before introducing the argument? *Accept reasonable answers that may include: to engage the reader, to show humpback whales have extraordinary physical qualities, to introduce the whales to the reader in a personal way.*

6. What does cleverness indicate? *Intelligence*

5

Humpbacks ❶seem to communicate with each other by making grunting and whistling sounds. These sounds are mostly made by mothers and ❸calves calling to each other, but members of a ❹pod also communicate with each other. Scientists do not yet know what all humpback sounds mean. ❺But some calls do seem to have particular uses and meanings.

6

Compared to their body size, humpback brains are smaller than those of humans, chimps, or dolphins. But scientists have found that their brains show another ❻sign of intelligence: they have a complex structure, or shape. The cortex, or outer part, of the humpback brain is deeply folded and made up of several layers, ❼in a similar way to a human brain.

7

❽Scientists have found cells called spindle cells in humpbacks and other whales' brains. They are thought to be used in language and understanding emotions. ❾The only other animals known to have them are humans, apes, chimpanzees, and elephants.

D 7. Why does the author use the word *seem? Intelligence is hard to measure, scientists think animals are intelligent and that they can communicate, but they can't prove it.*

8. What is the difference between the facts in the first three paragraphs and the "ideas" in paragraphs 4 and 5? *Paragraphs 1–3 contain facts that can be proven. The ideas are impressions—what scientists think is happening. Because intelligence is difficult to measure, it can only be assumed that the animals are exhibiting intelligence.*

E 9. What are *calves* in this context? *Elicit from context clues: baby humpback whales.*

F 10. What is a *pod* in this context? *Elicit from context clues: a group (herd, school) of humpback whales.*

G 11. What does *particular* mean in this context? *Elicit from context clues: distinctive among other examples of the same general category, specific.*

12. Why is it important that some of the calls seem to have particular uses and meanings? *They are specific rather than just random noises. The same noises are repeated by different animals with similar results or reactions or for the same reason. That is an indication that their sounds are more like a language, and they are communicating with each other at a higher level than animals that just make basic sounds without a particular use or meaning.*

H 13. Why is this a sign of intelligence? *The whale's brain has a structure similar to the human brain and both brains have the capacity for intelligence.*

I 14. What can you infer here? *If the structure of a whale's brain is similar to a human brain, and the animal is also exhibiting other types of intelligent behavior, the humpback whale may have similar human qualities.*

J 15. Why is this important? *Spindle cells are thought to be linked to language and emotion, both of which are signs of intelligence and characteristic of human behaviors.*

16. Why is this significant? *The presence of spindle cells in humpback whales is a specific detail that adds to the author's argument that humpbacks are intelligent and possess human-like qualities.*

K 17. Why is this important? *Most animals do not have spindle cells in their brains, which means that most animals do not have their own language, nor can they understand emotions. The only animals that have spindle cells are humans and other animals thought to be highly intelligent. Because humpback whales have spindle cells in their brains, they may have their own language and may understand emotions like humans do.*

18. What is the author doing in this paragraph? *The author is building her argument: Humpback whales have human characteristics that "seem" to show intelligence similar to human intelligence.*

8

Learning is a sign of intelligence. **❶**Like humans, humpbacks learn a lot as they grow up, instead of behaving mainly according to instinct from birth. **Ⓜ**Adult humpbacks also learn things from each other, such as new songs and new methods of hunting.

9

ⓃSome humpback whales use "bubble-net" feeding in groups. One or more whales swim in circles, blowing streams of bubbles that rise toward the surface in a ring. Others herd shoals of fish into the "bubble-net" this creates. Then, the humpbacks swim up inside the "net" to feed. **Ⓞ**The fish are afraid to swim out through the bubbles.

❶ 19. What is *instinct? Animal behavior that happens without prior experience (learning), such as nest building, migration, and finding food*

20. What does *instead of* imply? *Most animals are born with the ability to survive on their own. Instead of surviving on instinct, like most other animals, humpbacks are taught survival behaviors by their parents.*

21. How does this support the author's argument? *It is another example of a human characteristic in humpback whales. They show learned behavior like humans rather than instinctive behavior like most other (less intelligent) animals.*

Ⓜ 22. How is this similar to human behavior? *Adults teach each other new skills; that means the humpbacks keep learning throughout their lifetimes and create new behaviors like humans do. Animals relying only on instinct have a fixed pattern of behavior that does not change (or grow) throughout their lives.*

23. How does the way humpbacks learn suggest that they are intelligent? *They are like humans in that they are taught how to survive by their parents rather than through instinct. Also, like humans, adult humpbacks continue to learn from each other. Because learning is a human quality connected to intelligence and because the whales learn from each other, they are also intelligent.*

Ⓝ 24. What human thinking skills are shown in this method of fishing? *Turn and talk, then share out. Elicit higher-order thinking skills, such as: strategizing, collaborating, cooperating, delegating tasks, sequencing, innovating, rewarding.*

Ⓞ 25. What does the fish behavior suggest about their level of intelligence. *They do not have the thinking skills nor intelligence that the humpback whales seem to have.*

10

Bubble-net hunting can even be seen as an example of ⓟusing tools, another sign of high intelligence. Scientists think humpbacks' constantly changing songs show they have ⓠa culture, with shared social activities and creations. People who have encountered humpbacks often say the whales even seemed to ⓡwant to communicate with them.

11

Does intelligence make an animal more ⓢ"human"? Some people argue that chimps, whales, and other intelligent animals should not be hunted or harmed, since they are ⓣintelligent, like us. ⓤShould smart animals be treated better?

> CENTRAL IDEA: Humpback whales have human qualities and should be treated more "human(e)ly."

ⓟ 26. What tool do the whales use in bubble-net hunting? *The bubbles*

ⓠ 27. What is a *culture*? *Elicit that culture includes customs, beliefs, laws, art, and language of a nation or people.*

28. Is culture associated with animals? *Not usually. It is a human concept based on people living in groups.*

29. If scientists think humpback whales have a culture, what does that imply about their intelligence? *That it is high and they mirror human behaviors*

30. What are *creations*? *New activities and ideas; not just instinctive responses (human-like behavior)*

ⓡ 31. Why might whales seem to want to communicate? *Accept reasonable answers based on text evidence, such as: They see something in us that they recognize, they actually are highly intelligent and are curious about behaviors they see in humans.*

32. Is the author's argument convincing? Why or why not? *Turn and talk, then share out. Elicit that the argument seems convincing because there are so many examples of intelligent human-like behavior. These examples demonstrate that the humpback whales seem so smart and so human, which makes the argument so compelling.*

ⓢ 33. Why do authors use quotation marks around single words like this? *To show that the word is being used differently than it normally would be. The reader needs to think about how the word is being used in the context of the sentence.*

34. Why is *human* in quotes? *The author is not saying intelligent animals are human. She is saying they exhibit human-like behavior.*

ⓣ 35. Why shouldn't animals be hunted if they are "intelligent, like us"? *Turn and talk, then share out. Accept reasonable answers based on text evidence.*

ⓤ 36. Why does the author leave us with a question? *To make us think, to send a message, to make a statement, to state her claim*

37. Is there an answer to the question? *Turn and talk, then share out. Elicit that yes, the author thinks we should treat smart animals better.*

Humpback Whales:
ANNOTATED CONSTRUCTED RESPONSE EXEMPLARS

Recommended for Grades 4–6

Prompt: What does the author **really** want us to know about humpback whales?

Note: The following annotated exemplar is aligned with the Constructed Response Instructional Rubric Grades 3–4 (pages 155–156) and the Constructed Response Student Checklist Grades 3–4 (page 157).

Grade 4

The author wants us to know that we share many human-like qualities with humpback whales and that these very qualities should make us think about treating them more **Ⓐ**humanely. "Humpback whales, like other whales, have been seen doing some very clever things." The text tells us that whales communicate with each other using their own language. Some people even think whales have tried to communicate with them! If the language of whales is used to share thoughts, maybe this makes them more like us than we **Ⓑ**know. Scientists have found many similarities between human brains and those of humpback whales. They have found that humpback brains "have a complex structure, or shape. The cortex, or outer part, of the hump-back brain is deeply folded and made up of several layers, in a similar way to a human brain." If their brains are similar to ours it seems possible that they may be able to think like **Ⓒ**humans. According to the author, humpbacks are also capable of learning and not just acting by instinct like most other animals. "Like humans, humpbacks learn a lot as they grow up. Adult humpbacks also learn things from each other, such as new songs and new methods of hunting." One method of hunting they use is called "bubble-net hunting." The whales had to figure out a way to cooperate with one another to catch fish by surrounding the fish and tricking them into thinking they are caught in a net of bubbles. Humans cooperate to work together and it seems like whales **Ⓓ**do too. Evidence shows that humans and humpback whales communicate, have similar brains, and learn to share ideas. Maybe we should think more about our similarities than our **Ⓔ**differences. The author asks us to consider the question: "Should smart animals be treated better?" If humans are as smart as we think we are, we should be able to see how similar we are to humpbacks and recognize that treating them more human(e)ly is the right thing to **Ⓕ**do.

Ⓐ Answer/Central Idea

Ⓑ Text Evidence #1 with Rationale

Ⓒ Text Evidence #2 with Rationale

Ⓓ Text Evidence #3 with Rationale

Ⓔ Conclusion Part A

Ⓕ Conclusion Part B

Note: The following annotated exemplar is aligned with the Constructed Response Instructional Rubric Grades 5–8 (pages 158–159) and the Constructed Response Student Checklist Grades 5–8 (page 160).

Grades 5–6

The author wants us to know that we share many human-like qualities with humpback whales and that these very qualities should make us think about treating them more **G** humanely. "Humpback whales, like other whales, have been seen doing some very clever things." According to the text, humpback whales have even developed a way to communicate with one another. The ability to communicate is certainly thought of as a sign of intelligence, but actual language is thought of as a human quality. "People who have encountered humpbacks often say the whales even seemed to want to communicate with them." Communication is key to shared **H** thoughts. Scientists have found that humpback brains "have a complex structure, or shape. The cortex, or outer part of the humpback brain, is deeply folded and made up of several layers, in a similar way to a human brain." Scientists have even found spindle cells, thought to be used in language and understanding emotions, in the brains of humpbacks. If the structure of a humpback's brain is similar to a human brain, perhaps humpback whales are capable of thinking **I** similarly to humans. According to the author, humpbacks are also capable of learning and not just acting according to instinct like most other animals. "Like humans, humpbacks learn a lot as they grow up. Adult humpbacks also learn things from each other, such as new songs and new methods of hunting." In fact, one method of hunting used by humpbacks, bubble-net hunting, requires that the animals coordinate their efforts, communicate with one another, and cooperate to catch their prey. The text suggests that these abilities to share "social activities and creations" are a sign of the use of tools, further evidence that humpbacks share human qualities and **J** abilities. Humans communicate, learn, share social activities, and make use of tools in everyday life, like humpbacks. It seems the qualities we share with humpbacks make us more alike than we might have **K** thought. The author asks us to consider the question: "Should smart animals be treated better?" Should we treat humpbacks differently because they are "like us"? Maybe a sign of human intelligence would be a more humane treatment of humpback **L** whales.

G Answer/Thesis

H Text Evidence #1 Interwoven with Rationale

I Text Evidence #2 Interwoven with Rationale

J Text Evidence #3 Interwoven with Rationale

K Conclusion Part A

L Conclusion Part B

Medgar Evers
by Ann Weil

There are many heroes in U.S. history. These men and women risked their lives to make the country a better place for everyone. Medgar Evers was one of these heroes.

Evers was an African American, or black American, dedicated to the idea of racial justice at a time when blacks in his home state of Mississippi were far from free. During the period when Medgar grew up, life in southern states like Mississippi was very difficult for black people. Between 1877 and 1910, all southern states—and some northern ones—passed laws known as Jim Crow laws. These made black Americans second-class citizens. According to federal law, black people had the legal right to vote, but men with guns blocked them from voting. Blacks could not sit at a public lunch counter, nor could they swim at a public pool.

Segregation was in place in all public places. Schools, buses, hospitals, restaurants, parks, and even cemeteries were separated by race. The areas reserved for black people were older and shabbier than those for white people. Sometimes there were no areas for black people at all. Blacks had to use the back entrances to stores. They had to wait until all white customers had been served before it was their turn. They were not allowed to call white people by their first names.

The "American dream" of a better life seemed out of reach for southern blacks during this period. Their hard work did not seem to get them any closer. Still, white people in the South were totally dependent on blacks in order to maintain their lifestyle. Black laborers in the cotton fields made white plantation owners wealthy. Black women did the cooking and laundry for many white households. They also took care of the babies. And when a white person died, it was a black man who dug his or her grave.

Medgar Evers showed extraordinary courage by speaking out against a system of inequality that so many took for granted. His work to secure voting rights for black people inspired fear and hatred among white extremists, who wanted to keep blacks "in their place."

Evers' first job was to sell life insurance to blacks who lived in the Mississippi Delta. Evers and his wife moved to an all-black town called Mound Bayou. For his job, Evers drove all across the Mississippi Delta. These travels allowed Evers to see a new side of the black experience in Mississippi. Many of the people Evers saw were sharecroppers. These black farmers did not own their land as Evers' family had. Rather, they rented land from plantation owners. The plantation owners cheated the black sharecroppers out of any profits they might make. They also lived in some of the worst conditions of poverty Evers had ever seen.

Inspired by his experiences, Evers decided to work to bring the civil rights movement to Mississippi. Evers joined the National Association for the Advancement of Colored People (NAACP). The NAACP was started in 1909. A group of white people was horrified by the violence they saw against black Americans. They wanted to help blacks get equal protection under the law. There were about 60 founding members, both black and white. The organization grew over the years. By the 1950s there were more than half a million members all over the country.

Evers encouraged other blacks in Mississippi to join. This was one way he hoped to improve their lives.

In addition to investigating racial violence, Evers organized boycotts. He also encouraged nonviolent sit-ins. Blacks would sit down at a white-only lunch counter, or go to a white library and sit down there. Doing this took courage. They were often assaulted or arrested. Evers and other civil rights activists believed that such actions would help their cause.

During this period the southern whites in power did everything they could to keep blacks "in their place." Evers knew that this could only change if more blacks in Mississippi voted. But whites did not want blacks to vote. They targeted blacks who registered to vote with increasing violence. Evers always said he was working to make Mississippi a better place for all people, not just blacks. But many middle-class blacks in Mississippi did not appreciate what he was trying to do. They were afraid that his actions would stir up trouble. Some blacks even spied on Evers. They kept track of what he did and where he went. They even reported this to the police.

Evers' wife said, "Medgar knew what he was doing, and he knew what the risks were. He just decided that he had to do what he had to do. But I knew at some point in time that he would be taken from me."

Evers persisted in his work up until the day he was shot and killed outside his home in Mississippi on June 12, 1963. When he was assassinated, this made him one of the first martyrs of the civil rights movement. Medgar's wife sought justice for his murder. She also took up his fight to make Mississippi and the United States a better place for black Americans. Medgar Evers is remembered for his hard work and dedication to bringing civil rights to black Americans. He is remembered to have said, "You can kill a man, but you can't kill an idea."

Thanks to the sacrifices of people like Medgar Evers, equal rights for all races in the United States is no longer a dream.

Medgar Evers:
TEACHER DISCUSSION GUIDE
Grade Level: 4–6, Guided Reading Level: Q, Lexile Level: 800L

1

There are many **A**heroes in U.S. history. These men and women **B**risked their lives to make the country a better place for everyone. Medgar Evers was one of these heroes.

2

Evers was an African American, or black American, dedicated to the idea of **C**racial justice at a time when blacks in his home state of Mississippi were **D**far from free. During the period when Medgar grew up, life in southern states like Mississippi was very difficult for black people. Between 1877 and 1910, all southern states— and some northern ones—passed laws known as Jim Crow laws. These made black Americans **E**second-class citizens. According to federal law, black people had the legal right to vote, but men with guns blocked them from voting. Blacks could not sit at a public lunch counter, nor could they swim at a public pool.

A 1. What is a *hero? Turn and talk. Have students identify characteristics of a hero and share out with the class.*

B 2. What does it mean to *risk your life? Elicit that it means that despite knowing your life is in danger, you continue to work for something you truly believe in.*

3. Why did he have to risk his life to make the country a better place for all? *Many people thought he was too outspoken and that he was stirring up trouble needlessly. Many people, both black and white, were upset that he was trying to make things equal for all, and they were willing to fight (or kill) to stop it from happening.*

C 4. What is *justice? Elicit or share definition: fair and reasonable treatment.*

5. What is *racial justice? Fair and equal treatment for all races; extension of the same civil rights for all people, regardless of race*

6. Why was Evers' dedication to the idea of racial justice something he was willing to fight for? Why didn't everyone feel the way he did about wanting things to change? *Have students turn and talk. Accept reasonable, logical answers based on text evidence. Elicit that he was different from most, and he felt compelled to stand up. He was a hero.*

D 7. Far from free of what? *Far from the freedom to experience racial justice. This is a reference to blacks being free from slavery. White people in the South were angry that blacks had been given their freedom after the Civil War. Blacks were not free from the second-class citizenship that whites forced them into. They were not given the civil rights they were entitled to, so they were unable to experience the freedoms that white Americans had.*

E 8. What is a second-class citizen? *A person who is discriminated against despite being considered part of the population. Second-class citizens are refused rights, such as voting, sitting at public lunch counters, or swimming in public pools. Classifying specific groups of people in this way is considered a violation of human rights.*

9. Who were considered the "first-class" citizens? *The white people who were making the laws.*

3

F Segregation was in place in all public places. **G** Schools, buses, hospitals, restaurants, parks, and even cemeteries were separated by race. The areas reserved for black people were older and shabbier than those for white people. Sometimes there were no areas for black people at all. Blacks had to use the back entrances to stores. They had to wait until all white customers had been served before it was their turn. They were not allowed to call white people by their first names.

4

The **H** "American dream" of a better life seemed **I** out of reach for southern blacks during this period. Their hard work did not seem to get them any closer. **J** Still, white people in the South were totally dependent on blacks in order to maintain their lifestyle. Black laborers in the cotton fields made white plantation owners wealthy. Black women did the cooking and laundry for many white households. They also took care of the babies. And when a white person died, it was a black man who dug his or her grave.

5

Medgar Evers showed **K** extraordinary courage by speaking out against a **L** system of inequality that **M** so many took for granted. His work to secure voting rights for black people inspired fear and hatred among white extremists, **N** who wanted to keep blacks "in their place."

F 10. What is *segregation? Elicit from context clues: the practice of separating people of different races in schools, housing, and public or community places as a form of discrimination.*

G 11. Why did white people mistreat black people so horribly? *Refer to question 7. Whites were still recovering from changes made after the Civil War and did not want to consider former slaves their equals. They were discriminating due to their racial biases.*

H 12. What is the *American dream? The idea that all Americans, regardless of social class, have the right to make their lives rich and full through hard work and effort*

I 13. Why was it out of reach? *The Jim Crow laws put restrictions on African Americans that kept them working very hard, but prevented them from living the lives they wanted to have.*

J 14. What unusual situation is this author presenting here? *Whites were only able to maintain their first-class status because they forced second-class status onto the blacks who worked for them. White people treated the black people horribly, but could not maintain their lifestyle without them.*

K 15. Why did he show extraordinary courage by speaking out? *He put his life on the line from the beginning. No one else was objecting publicly to any of the injustices. He was going against the current situation, and he knew that was dangerous, yet he did it anyway.*

L 16. What was the system of inequality? *The system of separate and unequal; segregation and second-class citizenship*

M 17. Who took the system for granted? *Both blacks and whites; whites assumed blacks would stay "in their place" because of the laws, and many blacks were complaisant—they did not want to stir up trouble for themselves or make things worse than they already were.*

N 18. What were white extremists afraid of? *Turn and talk. Accept reasonable responses based on the text, such as: If blacks voted, they could change the laws to establish equal justice, and white extremists wanted things to remain the same in order to maintain their lifestyle—they could keep blacks doing what they wanted them to do.*

6

Evers' first job was to sell life insurance to blacks who lived in the Mississippi Delta. Evers and his wife moved to an all-black town called Mound Bayou. For his job, Evers drove all across the Mississippi Delta. These travels allowed Evers **O**to see a new side of the black experience in Mississippi. Many of the people Evers saw were sharecroppers. **P**These black farmers did not own their land as Evers' family had. Rather, they rented land from plantation owners. The plantation owners cheated the black sharecroppers out of any profits they might make. They also lived in some of the **Q**worst conditions of poverty Evers had ever seen.

7

RInspired by his experiences, Evers **S**decided to work to bring the civil rights **T**movement to Mississippi. Evers joined the National Association for the Advancement of **U**Colored People (NAACP). The NAACP was started in 1909. A group of white people was horrified by the violence they saw against black Americans. They wanted to help blacks get equal protection under the law. There were about 60 founding members, both black and white. The organization grew over the years. By the 1950s there were more than half a million members all over the country.

8

VEvers encouraged other blacks in Mississippi to join. This was one way he hoped to improve their lives.

9

In addition to investigating racial violence, Evers organized **W**boycotts. He also encouraged **X**nonviolent sit-ins. Blacks would sit down at a white-only lunch counter, or go to a white library and sit down there. **Y**Doing this took courage. They were often assaulted or arrested. Evers and other civil rights activists believed that such actions would help **Z**their cause.

O 19. What does it mean to see a new side? *To see something from a new perspective—to look at it differently than you did before*

P 20. What is the new side that Evers saw? *Evers had no idea how bad farming could be for sharecroppers because his family had owned their own land.*

Q 21. What caused the conditions of poverty? *Because of racial injustice, sharecroppers were cheated out of their profits. They worked hard, but could not reap the benefits of the American dream because of the inequality imposed by the Jim Crow laws.*

R 22. What is the meaning of *inspired* in this context? *To cause action, motivate. Evers felt like he had to do something about the situation.*

S 23. What did the inspiration cause Evers to do? *He decided to dedicate his life to bringing the civil rights movement to Mississippi.*

T 24. What is *a movement* in this context? *It is an idea, an ideology, shared by a group of people with a common goal for change.*

U 25. *Note: At your discretion discuss this terminology in the context of its historical reference.*

V 26. How would joining the movement improve people's lives? *Turn and talk. Accept reasonable responses based on text evidence, such as: more people/more power, more involved/more change, taking ownership/more investment in the cause.*

W 27. What is a *boycott*? *Elicit that it is refusing to buy products or services from or patronize businesses that exhibited racial injustice.*

X 28. What is a *nonviolent sit-in*? *Peacefully moving in, occupying space in a public place, and refusing to move in order to protest unfair treatment*

Y 29. What kind of courage did this take? *People would have to be brave and put the fear of harm to themselves to the side to help other people.*

Z 30. What was the cause? *To end segregation*

31. How did Evers think the boycotts and sit-ins would help their cause? *Turn and talk with a partner. Accept reasonable answers based on text evidence, such as: They drew attention to the problem, pointed out how inappropriate the laws were, etc.*

10

During this period the southern whites in power did everything they could to keep blacks "in their place." Evers knew that this could only change if more blacks in Mississippi voted. **A A** But whites did not want blacks to vote. They targeted blacks who registered to vote with increasing violence. Evers always said he was working to make Mississippi a better place for all people, not just blacks. But many middle-class blacks in Mississippi did not appreciate what he was trying to do. They were afraid that his actions would stir up trouble. Some blacks even spied on Evers. They kept track of what he did and where he went. They even reported this to the police.

11

Evers' wife said, "Medgar knew what he was doing, and he knew what the risks were. **B B** He just decided that he had to do what he had to do. But I knew at some point in time that he would be taken from me."

12

Evers persisted in his work up until the day he was **C C** shot and killed outside his home in Mississippi on June 12, 1963. When he was **D D** assassinated, this made him one of the first martyrs of the civil rights movement. Medgar's wife sought justice for his murder. She also took up his fight to make Mississippi and the United States a better place for black Americans. Medgar Evers is remembered for his hard work and dedication to bringing civil rights to black Americans. He is remembered to have said, **E E** "You can kill a man, but you can't kill an idea."

13

Thanks to the sacrifices of people like Medgar Evers, equal rights for all races in the United States is **F F** no longer a dream.

A A 32. Why didn't whites want blacks to vote? *They did not want to lose their power over blacks. They were afraid if black people voted, the racial injustice would end; white people wanted to maintain their superiority and the control of black people.*

B B 33. Why did he feel so compelled to continue his work? *He was a man who wanted to do the right thing in spite of the dangers. His cause meant so much to him, and he was willing to die rather than live with the prevailing injustices.*

34. What kind of people put themselves in harm's way for the sake of their beliefs? *Heroes, martyrs, people of conviction*

35. Why do they do it? *They are made of different "stuff" and that sets them apart. They want something better, not just for themselves, but for their children, and they see things differently because they see outside of themselves.*

C C 36. Why did someone want to kill Medgar Evers? *Turn and talk. Accept reasonable responses based on text evidence, including: He was making both blacks and whites angry, people on both sides were resorting to violence to stop things from changing, he wouldn't give up even when people asked him to.*

D D 37. What is a *martyr? A person who is killed for his or her beliefs*

38. Why is Medgar Evers considered a martyr of the civil rights movement? *He gave his life for the cause.*

39. The author states that Medgar Evers is a hero. Why is he a hero in the author's eyes? *He was a man who stood up for his beliefs. Even though many people were against him, he never gave up, he wanted to help society, he left a lasting impression that still lives on, and he died for his beliefs.*

40. Revisit student definitions of a hero from the beginning of the lesson. Does Medgar Evans fit their definitions? *Students may want to revise or add to their original definitions based on the author's point of view.*

E E 41. What did Evers mean by this? *You can stop me, but you can't stop what I stand for. My principles and dreams will live on in others after I'm gone.*

F F 42. Why isn't it just a dream? *Evers' work led to the success of the civil rights movement and the end of segregation in the South.*

CENTRAL IDEA: Medgar Evers was a hero because he made a choice to make a difference knowing he was putting himself in danger by doing so.

Medgar Evers:
ANNOTATED CONSTRUCTED RESPONSE EXEMPLARS

Recommended for Grades 4–6

Prompt: What does the author **really** want us to know about Medgar Evers?

Note: The following annotated exemplar is aligned with the Constructed Response Instructional Rubric Grades 3–4 (pages 155–156) and the Constructed Response Student Checklist Grades 3–4 (page 157).

Grade 4

The author wants us to know that Medgar Evers was a hero because he made a personal decision to dedicate his life to achieving equal rights for African Americans, and he lost his life in the **(A)** process. He "showed extraordinary courage by speaking out against a system of inequality that so many took for granted." Evers couldn't take things for granted. He stood up for what he believed in when no one else would. It takes a certain kind of a person to do that—a **(B)** hero. When he saw the horrible conditions black sharecroppers were living in after being cheated out of their profits by white plantation owners, with no hope for a better future, he "decided to work to bring the civil rights movement to Mississippi." He made a choice to help African Americans through his work with the NAACP. He wanted to improve

(A) Answer/Central Idea

(B) Text Evidence #1 with Rationale

(C) Text Evidence #2 with Rationale

(D) Text Evidence #1 with Rationale

(E) Conclusion Part A

(F) Conclusion Part B

their lives by helping to make the "American dream" easier for them to **(C)** achieve. He also wanted to stop segregation. He "organized boycotts" and "encouraged nonviolent sit-ins" in which he and other blacks sat at white-only lunch counters and went into white-only libraries. This was a brave thing to do because he knew he could be "assaulted or arrested," but he did it anyway to help the cause. "Medgar knew what he was doing, and he knew what the risks were," but standing up for what he believed in was more important to him than anything else, and that was **(D)** heroic. Medgar Evers saw something wrong with the world and lost his life trying to make it right. He was motivated by his desire to make changes for the good of all people, and he went to great lengths for what he believed in. That's what heroes **(E)** do. The author wants us to know that Medgar Evers was a man who sacrificed his life for what he believed in. He himself said, "You can kill a man, but you can't kill an idea," and in a way he was predicting his own future. His ideas did not die with him. They continue to live in the hearts and minds of the many Americans who benefited from his belief that all people, black or white, deserve a chance to make a better life for **(F)** themselves.

Note: The following annotated exemplar is aligned with the Constructed Response Instructional Rubric Grades 5–8 (pages 158–159) and the Constructed Response Student Checklist Grades 5–8 (page 160).

Grades 5–6

The author wants us to know that Medgar Evers was a man who stood up for what he believed in regardless of the possible risks to himself, and as a result of his efforts, is considered a hero of the civil rights **G** movement. "Evers was an African American dedicated to the idea of racial justice" at a time when Jim Crow laws "made black Americans second-class citizens." Evers' dedication to the idea of helping African Americans pursue the "American dream" and equal rights led him to actions that were risky and even life threatening. Evers routinely put his ideals before his own personal safety to highlight his cause and make **H** changes. "Medgar Evers showed extraordinary courage by speaking out against a system of inequality that so many blacks took for granted. His work to secure voting rights for black people inspired fear and hatred among white extremists, who wanted to keep blacks 'in their place.' … men with guns blocked them from voting." For most people, the risk of personal harm may be too high a price to pay for a cause, but this was not the case for Evers. His conviction to his cause drove him to boycotting establishments refusing equal rights to blacks and risking his own safety and potentially his **I** life. "During this period the southern whites in power did everything they could to keep blacks 'in their place.' Evers knew that this could only change if more blacks in Mississippi voted. But whites did not want blacks to vote. They targeted blacks who registered to vote with increasing violence." Violence against blacks daring to challenge injustice was frequent and many were afraid to join the movement. Evers knew his increasing involvement in the civil rights movement made him a target of white extremists, but he refused to be stopped in his pursuit of equal rights. According to his wife, "Medgar knew what he was doing, and he knew what the risks were. He just decided to do what he had to **J** do." Evers had the moral conviction to do what was right even in the face of personal danger. These heroic actions cost him his life when he was assassinated in June 1963, making him "one of the first martyrs of the civil rights movement." Medgar Evers made the ultimate sacrifice for what he believed in, giving his life in the pursuit of a better life for African Americans, making him a true American **K** hero. Faced with the decision to stand up for what is right is often hard, but heroes such as Medgar Evers provide an inspiration and a reminder that many positive changes in our society have come as the result of the hard work and dedication of men and women willing to fight for a **L** cause.

G Answer/Thesis

H Text Evidence #1 Interwoven with Rationale

I Text Evidence #2 Interwoven with Rationale

J Text Evidence #3 Interwoven with Rationale

K Conclusion Part A

L Conclusion Part B

A Profound Legacy from *Mesopotamia*

by Don Nardo

1

Iraq—the site of ancient Mesopotamia—officially became a nation in the 1930s. At the time, like many other Middle Eastern countries, it was poor, and its people had few machines and other advances. People living in Western nations looked on the area as backward and unimportant.

2

In part this was because many aspects of everyday life in the former Mesopotamia had undergone little or no change since ancient times. A striking example was a typical street market. After excavating ancient Sumerian and Babylonian markets, archaeologists noticed something remarkable. The ancient markets were nearly identical to modern Iraqi ones. Both were filled with makeshift merchants' booths that had cloth awnings to shield people from the hot sun. The old and new versions alike lacked electricity, running water, and other conveniences.

3

In addition, early modern Iraq city dwellers lived in houses much like the small mud-brick ones of their ancient ancestors. The same was true of the inhabitants of the broad marshes stretching across sections of southern Iraq. The ancient marsh dwellers built their houses from the reeds that grow in the Tigris and Euphrates rivers. As late as the 1970s, many rural Iraqis erected identical reed huts. Also like their ancient counterparts, the Iraqi marsh dwellers used small boats fashioned from reeds. Similarly, the men and boys still enjoyed a game that originated in Sumer nearly 60 centuries ago. The players stood in their boats and tried to push their opponents into the water.

> A Profound Legacy from *Mesopotamia*

Well into the 20th century, Iraq was a place where past and present met daily. Its technology and living standards remained far behind those of Western nations. Few people in the West were aware of Iraq's glorious past. Nor did they appreciate the huge cultural debt they owed to the peoples and nations of ancient Mesopotamia.

Today the significance of that huge debt is better understood. It is widely known that some of the first forms of agriculture began in the hills overlooking the Mesopotamian plains. Later, the first cities sprang up on those plains.

The first governments were formed to run those cities. The cities were also where writing was invented and some of the first schools were established. Other firsts established by the Sumerians and their immediate successors were irrigation canals, roads, religious temples, written laws and courts, charts showing the stars and planets, and the concept of kings receiving divine authority to rule.

7

These and other civilized advances steadily spread outward from ancient Mesopotamia to other parts of the globe. Peoples in India, Europe, and Africa felt their influence. They absorbed the ideas, making them their own, and then they passed them along to others. This slow but relentless process is called cultural diffusion. It continued through many centuries and countless generations until Mesopotamia's profound legacy reached the present day. In a surprising number of ways, it helped to make the author of this book, along with all of its readers, who we are.

A Profound Legacy from *Mesopotamia:*
TEACHER DISCUSSION GUIDE

Grade Level: 5–6, Guided Reading Level: U, Lexile Level: 1000L

1

Iraq—**A**the site of ancient Mesopotamia—officially became a nation in the 1930s. At the time, like many other Middle Eastern countries, it was poor, and its people had few machines and other advances. People living in Western nations looked on the area as **B**backward and unimportant.

2

CIn part this was because many aspects of everyday life in the former Mesopotamia had undergone little or no change since ancient times. A striking example was a typical street market. After excavating ancient Sumerian and Babylonian markets, archaeologists noticed something **D**remarkable. The ancient markets were nearly identical to modern Iraqi ones. Both were filled with makeshift merchants' booths that had cloth awnings to shield people from the hot sun. The old and new versions alike lacked electricity, running water, and other conveniences.

3

In addition, early modern Iraq city dwellers lived in houses much like the small mud-brick ones of their ancient ancestors. The same was true of the inhabitants of the broad marshes stretching across sections of southern Iraq. The ancient marsh dwellers built their houses from the reeds that grow in the Tigris and Euphrates rivers. **E**As late as the 1970s, many rural Iraqis

A 1. What does this mean? *The modern country of Iraq is located in the same place that ancient Mesopotamia was located.*

B 2. Why would Western nations think Iraq was backward? *It was a poor country without societal advances.*

C 3. What is the author saying about the Western perspective of Iraq being backward? *That it was understandable.*

D 4. What was remarkable about their findings? *The old and the new were the same. Usually an ancient excavation yields artifacts that differ from and are less advanced than modern ones.*

E 5. What evidence does the author present to support the idea that Iraq maintains its tradition of ancient practices and culture? *Houses in modern cities and rural areas were built the same way ancient houses were, without modern conveniences or technology. Their boats were made of reeds rather than more modern materials, they played games that had been popular for thousands of years.*

erected identical reed huts. Also like their ancient counterparts, the Iraqi marsh dwellers used small boats fashioned from reeds. **F**Similarly, the men and boys still enjoyed a game that originated in Sumer nearly 60 centuries ago. The players stood in their boats and tried to push their opponents into the water.

4

GWell into the 20th century, Iraq was a place where past and present met daily. Its technology and living standards remained far behind those of Western nations. Few people in the West were aware of **H**Iraq's glorious past. Nor did they appreciate the **I**huge cultural debt they owed to the peoples and nations of ancient Mesopotamia.

5

JToday the significance of that huge debt is better understood. It is widely known that some of the first forms of agriculture began in the hills overlooking the Mesopotamian plains. Later, the first cities sprang up on those plains.

6

The first governments were formed to run those cities. The cities were also where writing was invented and some of the first schools were established. Other firsts established by the Sumerians and their immediate successors were irrigation canals, roads, religious temples, written laws and courts, charts showing the stars and planets, and the concept of kings receiving divine authority to rule.

7

These and other **K**civilized advances steadily spread outward from ancient Mesopotamia to other parts of the **L**globe. Peoples in India, Europe, and Africa felt their

F 6. How is this detail different from the others in the paragraph? *It provides information about traditional pastimes rather than traditional methods of building shelter and transportation.*

7. Why did the author include it? *It introduces the idea of celebrating the society and its traditions. Iraq may be lagging behind, but the men and boys are choosing to play and enjoy a game that originated with their ancestors. They have held onto something of cultural importance that links the old with the new and demonstrates an appreciation for their past.*

G 8. How is this different from other societies, especially Western ones? *It shows that in Iraq, the past and present are one and the same. In most Western societies there are elements of the past mixed in with the present, but mixing the two isn't as common.*

H 9. What is the glorious past that Westerners are unaware of? *The people of Mesopotamia and all it stood for were ancestors of the Iraqi people.*

I 10. What is the huge cultural debt the West owes to ancient Mesopotamia? *See examples of "firsts" in paragraphs 5 and 6.*

11. Why should we be thankful for all of these "firsts"? *Because they formed the foundation of modern society*

J 12. Why is the significance of the debt better understood today? *Because of the excavations and discoveries made by archaeologists*

K 13. Why are the advances considered civilized? *Because they helped build civilizations—cooperative, functioning societies*

L 14. What is the meaning of *globe* in this context? *Elicit from context clues: Earth, the world, the planet.*

influence. **ⓜ**They absorbed the ideas, making them their own, and then they passed them along to others. This slow but relentless process is called **ⓝ**cultural diffusion. It continued through many centuries and countless generations until Mesopotamia's **ⓞ**profound legacy reached the present day. **ⓟ**In a surprising number of ways, **ⓠ**it helped to make the author of this book, along with all of its readers, who we are.

CENTRAL IDEA:
Mesopotamia's profound legacy has formed the cornerstones of civilized societies around the world.

ⓜ 15. How can a culture absorb ideas? *Add the new ideas to the established culture to develop societal advances*

16. How does a culture make new ideas "their own"? *When new ideas are absorbed and blended with an established culture, something new is created. The new idea eventually becomes part of the established culture and is then considered "its own."*

17. How are the new ideas passed along to others? *Through word of mouth, travel, trade, etc.*

ⓝ 18. What does *diffusion* mean? *Elicit from context clues: spreading out, dispersing.*

19. What is *cultural diffusion? The slow and persistent process of spreading ideas and advancements from people to people and from country to country*

20. Why is it a relentless process? *Because it is never-ending. As new advancements are made, they are shared, built upon, and infused into societies all around the globe. Because new advancements are constantly discovered, the cycle continues.*

ⓞ 21. What is a *legacy? Elicit or define: something handed down from the past.*

22. What is Mesopotamia's legacy? *Mesopotamia is considered the birthplace of civilization. Its agricultural advancements led to people living in cities, which led to organized governments and established cultures. The ideas passed from generation to generation have greatly influenced present-day societies.*

23. What does *profound* mean? *Elicit or define: far-reaching, extensive, sweeping.*

24. Why does the author say Mesopotamia's legacy is profound? *Because through cultural diffusion, Mesopotamia's societal advancements have been shared, improved upon, and welcomed by most peoples of the world today, especially in the West.*

25. Revisit the last sentence in paragraph 1. Why did Westerners think Iraq was unimportant? *Because they didn't realize Iraq was the site of ancient Mesopotamia—an archaeological treasure trove.*

26. Why is that ironic? *Iraq is a nation stuck in the past. It has not progressed like the rest of the world, yet it sits atop the birthplace of Western civilization. Westerners looked down on a modern country they considered backward not realizing they would be as "forward" as they are.*

ⓟ 27. Why does the author write *a surprising number of ways? Before the breadth of Mesopotamia's profound legacy was made clear in the text, readers might not have realized how influential it truly was.*

ⓠ 28. What does this mean? *Turn and talk to a partner. Elicit that the profound legacy of Mesopotamia has crossed generations, cultures, and continents to form the foundations of modern societies all around the world.*

A Profound Legacy from *Mesopotamia:*
ANNOTATED CONSTRUCTED RESPONSE EXEMPLAR

Recommended for Grades 5–6

Prompt: What does the author **really** want us to know about Mesopotamia's legacy?

Note: The following annotated exemplar is aligned with the Constructed Response Instructional Rubric Grades 5–8 (pages 158–159) and the Constructed Response Student Checklist Grades 5–8 (page 160).

The author wants us to know that Mesopotamia's legacy is so profound that even though the society is ancient, through cultural diffusion, it has influenced modern societies throughout the **Ⓐ**world. "Few people in the West were aware of Iraq's glorious past. Nor did they appreciate the huge cultural debt they owed to the peoples and nations of ancient Mesopotamia." Before archaeologists unearthed ancient artifacts from the land where Iraq now stands, modern societies in the West were unaware that Mesopotamia's legacy had influenced them so greatly. Thanks to what was excavated and also to the evidence found in modern-day Iraq, this debt is much better **Ⓑ**understood. Many aspects of modern societies originated in Mesopotamia. "The first forms of agriculture … the first cities … the first governments… " all date to Mesopotamia and are only part of what makes up the huge cultural debt we owe its people. Additionally, we can thank Mesopotamia for the invention of writing, the first schools, written laws, and many other things that are major pieces of many modern **Ⓒ**cultures. The legacy of Mesopotamia was brought to present day through cultural diffusion. The firsts "steadily spread outward from ancient Mesopotamia to other parts of the globe." Once people found out about the "civilized advances," they welcomed them in their societies and then "passed them along to others." The ideas were passed along over and over again for many generations and for many, many years. Eventually, the influences and innovations of Mesopotamia reached modern times and formed the foundation of the modern societies we are familiar with **Ⓓ**today. The author wants us to know that the gifts Mesopotamia gave us are profound because they are so far-reaching and so widespread. The legacy of Mesopotamia has been brought to us through cultural diffusion, and as the author says, helped make all of us "who we **Ⓔ**are." Despite the perception of modern-day Iraq, and the irony that it sits atop the remnants of an ancient culture, the modern world owes its people a debt of gratitude. The author also wants us to know that we need to celebrate Iraq's glorious past because it has, "in a surprising number of ways," touched all of **Ⓕ**us.

Ⓐ Answer/Thesis

Ⓑ Text Evidence #1 Interwoven with Rationale

Ⓒ Text Evidence #2 Interwoven with Rationale

Ⓓ Text Evidence #3 Interwoven with Rationale

Ⓔ Conclusion Part A

Ⓕ Conclusion Part B

Man on the Moon
by Pamela Dell

1 Had the president lost his mind? Many people had to wonder when President John F. Kennedy spoke to Congress on May 25, 1961. "I believe this nation," he said, "should commit itself to achieving the goal, before this decade is out, of landing a man on the moon and returning him safely to Earth."

2 Some Americans thought the president's idea was the most unrealistic thing they'd ever heard. But others believed it was possible and strongly wanted to see it happen. Four years earlier the Soviet Union had caught the United States by surprise with its own space success story.

3 The event that took America by surprise occurred October 4, 1957. That day the Soviets launched a satellite into space. Called *Sputnik 1,* it was the first artificial satellite to orbit Earth. The beach-ball-sized object circled the globe once, a journey that took only 96 minutes.

4 Just one month later, *Sputnik 2* followed *Sputnik 1* into space. This was an even more impressive feat. *Sputnik 2* carried much heavier cargo—including Laika, a very-much-alive dog. The two successful spacecraft launches brought pride to the Soviet Union. Premier Nikita Khrushchev boasted about the Communist triumph over the democratic system in the United States.

5 In July 1955, two years before the Soviet satellite launches, the American government had announced plans for a similar mission. By 1957 the goal was near. But with the successful Sputnik missions, the Soviet Union had beaten the United States to the accomplishment—and with larger, better satellites than the one the U.S. was building. News of the two Sputnik voyages awed people around the world. But in America, it came as a shock—and sparked an international rivalry.

6 The Soviet Union was a large, powerful Communist country. That made it America's biggest enemy. Further, the United States prided itself on its technological know-how. With the Sputnik launches, it had suddenly been shown up as "second best." The desire to outdo the Soviet Union energized the nation. Americans wanted to see their country achieve bigger and better things in space—and to do them first. To many people, beating the Soviet Union also would symbolize the superiority of democracy over communism. The Sputnik launches accelerated the U.S. space program. What came to be called the space race was on.

7

Numerous other Soviet and American missions took place over the next few years. The rivalry intensified, and the American public was enthusiastically behind the space race. President Kennedy consulted with top experts in the space program and pressured them to come up with a space program that could be successfully accomplished before the Soviets could manage the same thing. After careful consideration of all the possibilities, one option stood out. Sending men to the moon, the experts agreed, was the way to go.

8

The three-man Apollo 11 crew blasted off from Cape Kennedy, Florida, at 9:32 a.m. Eastern time on July 16, 1969. After the spacecraft had orbited Earth one and a half times, the engines of the Saturn V rocket that had launched it into space fired again.

9

This shot the two-part spacecraft out of the earth's orbit and on its way to the moon, a journey of more than 235,000 miles. The astronauts, Neil Armstrong, Buzz Aldrin, and Michael Collins, rode in the command module, called *Columbia*. Attached to it was *Eagle,* the lunar module that would land on the moon.

10

It was 4:18 p.m. Eastern time on July 20, 1969, when the *Eagle* touched down on the moon's surface. It had been only four days since Apollo 11's liftoff from Earth. Immediately, Armstrong reported back to Mission Control in Houston, Texas. What he said has echoed through history: "The Eagle has landed."

11

After many hours of preparation, Armstrong finally left *Eagle*. On the way down the ladder attached to the landing gear, he pulled a cord that caused an on-board TV camera to begin recording him. As the camera rolled, Armstrong cautiously descended. With the world watching the live television broadcast, Armstrong spoke a few now-historic words. He said, "That's one small step for a man, one giant leap for mankind." A monumental achievement had occurred. Although live video of the first walk on the moon was being televised on Earth, Armstrong and Aldrin also had small regular film cameras to capture their experience in photographs.

12 One of those photos, known as AS11-40-5903, has become legendary. The faceless spaceman, Buzz Aldrin, is not recognizable because of the shiny protective visor that covers his entire face. A closer look at the visor reveals more information. Here the viewer sees a strange futuristic scene: Aldrin's long, dark shadow in the foreground, and in the distance, standing beside the shining lunar module, is another white-suited figure. It is Neil Armstrong, the photographer himself. Using the reflected image in the visor was the only way the two astronauts could capture themselves in a still photograph.

13 Photography is a powerful medium. Since the time of the earliest human beings, people's minds have been struck by the power of certain real-life scenes. But only through the use of cameras can moments be frozen in time, without recreation, to be viewed long after the moment they occurred.

14 Every photograph depicts a single moment of course, but in some of those single moments a whole story can be found. In some cases the image of the moment caught on film can represent much more than simply what's going on in the picture. This was certainly the case with the image of Aldrin on the moon. It showed a bizarre-looking figure, suited up for space and standing in a shallow crater. Behind him the black sky and the rocky, desolate landscape emphasized the stark strangeness of his location. On the astronaut's left shoulder was a patch of color that could not be missed. It was a red, white, and blue emblem of the flag of the United States of America. This photo was not just an image of someone named Buzz Aldrin wearing a spacesuit. To people in every country on Earth, it represented, and still represents, much more.

15 Here was a man who was more than 235,000 miles from our planet. He and one other crew member had reached another world. It was a photograph that told many stories, an image with various possible meanings. The most obvious was of course, how far, both literally and figuratively, the human race had come since its beginnings. The photograph also gave people hope for the future. If humans could land on the moon, then surely anything was possible. For some though, the most important meaning of the photograph was that the man in the picture came from the United States.

16 The Buzz Aldrin image we know as AS11-40-5903 will remain one of the most powerful existing representations of the achievements of humankind. Because of its bizarre beauty, its symbolic significance, and its widespread recognition as a major cultural marker, it will continue to inspire people to achieve great things, and it will long outlive the era in which it came to be.

Man on the Moon:
TEACHER DISCUSSION GUIDE

Grade Level: 5–7, Guided Reading Level: W, Lexile Level: 1050L

1

ⒶHad the president lost his mind? Many people had to wonder when President John F. Kennedy spoke to Congress on May 25, 1961. "I believe this nation," he said, "should commit itself to achieving the goal, before this decade is out, of landing a man on the moon and returning him safely to Earth."

2

ⒷSome Americans thought the president's idea was the most unrealistic thing they'd ever heard. But others believed it was possible and strongly wanted to see it happen. Four years earlier **Ⓒ**the Soviet Union had caught the United States by **Ⓓ**surprise with its own space success story.

3

The event that took America by surprise occurred October 4, 1957. That day the Soviets launched a satellite into space. Called *Sputnik 1*, it was the first **Ⓔ**artificial satellite to orbit Earth. The beach-ball-sized object circled the globe once, a journey that took only 96 minutes.

4

Just one month later, *Sputnik 2* followed *Sputnik 1* into space. This was an even more impressive feat. *Sputnik 2* carried much heavier cargo—including Laika, a very-much-alive dog. The two successful spacecraft launches brought pride to the Soviet Union. Premier Nikita Khrushchev **Ⓕ**boasted about the Communist triumph over the democratic system in the United States.

5

In July 1955, two years before the Soviet satellite launches, the American government had announced plans for a similar mission. By 1957 the goal was near. But with the successful Sputnik missions, the Soviet Union had beaten the United States to the accomplishment—and with larger, better satellites than the one the U.S. was building. News of the two Sputnik voyages awed people around the world. But in America, **Ⓖ**it came as a shock—and **Ⓗ**sparked an international rivalry.

Ⓐ 1. Why would people think the president had lost his mind? *The idea of sending a man to the moon and back seemed far-fetched and impossible.*

Ⓑ 2. Why did some people think a moon landing was so unrealistic? *It had never been done before, it was such a new concept, they didn't understand the president's motivation.*

Ⓒ 3. What was the Soviet Union? *Elicit or explain: a former country (1922–1991) made up of 15 Soviet republics ruled by the Communist Party. In its prime, it was the largest country in the world and competed with the United States for world power. The capital was Moscow, which is now the capital of Russia, one of the original 15 republics.*

4. Why did some people support the idea? *They understood the president's motivation, they thought it might be possible, they wanted to outshine the Soviets.*

Ⓓ 5. Why would the United States have been caught by surprise? *The Soviets had kept their space exploration plans a secret.*

Ⓔ 6. What is an *artificial satellite? An artificial object that has been put into orbit around Earth. The moon is a natural satellite of Earth.*

Ⓕ 7. Why was he boasting? *See paragraph 5: He was proud that his country had not only beaten the United States with the first satellite in orbit, it had also built larger and better satellites than the United States had.*

Ⓖ 8. Why was it a shock to Americans? *The Soviets had kept plans for the two launches a secret, and they were both very successful flights.*

Ⓗ 9. What is a *rivalry? Elicit from context clues: competition for superiority in a common goal.*

10. What does *international* mean in this context? *Elicit from context clues and word parts: between two nations—America and the Soviet Union.*

11. What were the United States and the Soviet Union competing for? *See paragraph 6: to be a number-one world power and number one in space technology and to prove that democracy was superior to communism or vice versa.*

12. How did the success of *Sputniks 1* and *2* spark an international rivalry? *Both countries thought dominance in space would prove that they were the number-one world power.*

6

The Soviet Union was a large, powerful Communist country. That made it America's biggest enemy. Further, the United States prided itself on its technological know-how. With the Sputnik launches, it had suddenly been shown up as "second best." The desire to outdo the Soviet Union energized the nation. Americans wanted to see their country achieve bigger and better things in space—and to do them first. To many people, beating the Soviet Union also would symbolize the superiority of democracy over communism. The Sputnik launches accelerated the U.S. space program. What came to be called the space race was on.

7

Numerous other Soviet and American missions took place over the next few years. The rivalry intensified, and the American public was enthusiastically behind the **I** space race. President Kennedy consulted with top experts in the space program and **J** pressured them to come up with a space program that could be successfully accomplished before the Soviets could manage the same thing. After careful consideration of all the possibilities, one option stood out. Sending men to the moon, the experts agreed, **K** was the way to go.

8

The three-man Apollo 11 crew blasted off from Cape Kennedy, Florida, at 9:32 a.m. Eastern time on July 16, 1969. After the spacecraft had orbited Earth one and a half times, the engines of the Saturn V rocket that had launched it into space fired again.

9

This shot the two-part spacecraft out of the Earth's orbit and on its way to the moon, a journey of more than 235,000 miles. The astronauts, Neil Armstrong, Buzz Aldrin, and Michael Collins, rode in the command module, called *Columbia*. Attached to it was **L** *Eagle*, the lunar module that would land on the moon.

10

It was 4:18 p.m. Eastern time on July 20, 1969, when the *Eagle* touched down on the moon's surface. It had been only four days since Apollo 11's liftoff from Earth. Immediately, Armstrong reported back to Mission Control in Houston, Texas. What he said has echoed through history: **M** "The Eagle has landed."

I 13. Why was it called a space race? *The two countries were in a race to see who could conquer outer space.*

14. Why was the American public supporting the competition? *Elicit that it was because of patriotism, dislike for the Soviets, and competitive spirit.*

J 15. Why would the president pressure them? *He was the leader of the space race, and he wanted to win. It would make him and the United States look weak if the Soviets won.*

K 16. Why did they choose a moon landing as the goal? *Turn and talk. Accept reasonable answers based on text evidence, including: It seemed attainable, it would give America control of the closest celestial body, it would be impressive, nothing could top it.*

L 17. Why is this symbolic? *The eagle is the national symbol of the United States.*

M 18. What does this imply? *Literally: The Eagle (a bird/the lunar module) has landed from its flight. Figuratively: The United States has landed on the moon.*

11

After many hours of preparation, Armstrong finally left *Eagle*. On the way down the ladder attached to the landing gear, he pulled a cord that caused an on-board TV camera to **N** begin recording him. As the camera rolled, Armstrong cautiously descended. With the world watching the live television broadcast, Armstrong spoke a few now-historic words. He said, **O** "That's one small step for a man, one giant leap for mankind." A monumental achievement had occurred. Although live video of the first walk on the moon was being televised on Earth, Armstrong and Aldrin also **P** had small regular film cameras to capture their experience in photographs.

12

Q One of those photos, known as AS11-40-5903, has become legendary. The faceless spaceman, Buzz Aldrin, is not recognizable because of the shiny protective visor that covers his entire face. A closer look at the visor reveals more information. Here the viewer sees a strange futuristic scene: Aldrin's long, dark shadow in the foreground, and in the distance, standing beside the shining lunar module, is another white-suited figure. It is Neil Armstrong, the photographer himself. **R** Using the reflected image in the visor was the only way the two astronauts could capture themselves in a still photograph.

13

S Photography is a powerful medium. Since the time of the earliest human beings, people's minds have been struck by the **T** power of certain real-life scenes. But only through the use of cameras can moments be **U** frozen in time, without recreation, to be viewed long after the moment they occurred.

N 19. Why was it important to record the event? *It was historic, it had seemed impossible, many people could watch it repeatedly.*

O 20. What does this mean? *His one step on the moon represents a monumental feat for all men (humanity). Elicit that he is not claiming the moon or the mission for himself, he is including everyone who was involved in the effort (all of humanity, including the Soviets) in the celebration. Despite international rivalry and winning the competition, his statement is one of peace and goodwill.*

P 21. What is a *regular film camera? Elicit or explain: Before digital cameras, film was used to capture photographic images. A regular film camera would take still film shots as opposed to the live video shots being streamed to Earth.*

22. Why did they also want to take photos? *To capture the moment clearly*

Q 23. Why has the photo become legendary? *Turn and talk. Accept reasonable answers based on text evidence, such as: It represented an incredible accomplishment, it was seen around the world, it represented the potential for unlimited possibilities.*

R 24. *This needs to be clarified. Elicit from students or explain: The reflected image was of the photographer. Both astronauts are shown in the photo—the subject of the photo and the photographer in the reflection from the subject's visor. This is similar to taking a selfie in a mirror; the reflection captures the photographer.*

S 25. How does the tone of the text change here? *From narrative (emotional, relaying a real event) to argumentative (matter of fact, presenting a point of view)*

26. What is a *medium as it is used in this context? A material used to create a work of art such as paint, metal, wood, etc. In this case, film is the medium that was used to produce the photo.*

T 27. How were real-life scenes depicted before we had photography? *Accept reasonable answers, such as: drawings, etchings, prints.*

U 28. What is the difference between drawings of real-life scenes and photographs that capture them? *Photos capture what is happening at the moment they are taken—what was really seen. Other depictions "re-create" what happened and can be influenced by a memory or an interpretation. Photographs freeze what actually happened so that the scene can be analyzed, reflected on, and recognized for what it really was.*

14

Every photograph depicts a single moment of course, but in some of those single moments a whole story can be found. In some cases the image of the moment caught on film can represent much more than simply what's going on in the picture. This was certainly the case with the image of Aldrin on the moon. It showed a bizarre-looking figure, suited up for space and standing in a shallow crater. Behind him the black sky and the rocky, desolate landscape emphasized the **ⓥ**stark strangeness of his location. On the astronaut's left shoulder was a patch of color that could not be missed. **ⓦ**It was a red, white, and blue emblem of the flag of the United States of America. This photo was not just an image of someone named Buzz Aldrin wearing a spacesuit. **ⓧ**To people in every country on Earth, it represented, and still represents, much more.

15

Here was a man who was more than 235,000 miles from our planet. He and one other crew member had reached another world. It was a photograph that told many stories, an **ⓨ**image with various possible meanings. **ⓩ**The most obvious was of course, how far, both literally and figuratively, the human race had come since its beginnings. The photograph also gave people hope for the future. If humans could land on the moon, then surely anything was **ⒶⒶ**possible. **ⒷⒷ**For some though, the most important meaning of the photograph was that the man in the picture came from the United States.

ⓥ 29. What does *stark* mean? *Elicit from context clues: barren, bleak, vacant.*

ⓦ 30. Why is this an important detail from the photograph? *It reflects both patriotism and nationalism and symbolizes the U.S. victory over the Soviet Union. It could not be missed because it was the only color in the photo.*

ⓧ 31. Why were people all over the world affected by the photograph? *It was such an amazing thing to have accomplished. It didn't matter who landed on the moon, it was astonishing that anyone could do what was thought to be impossible.*

32. What did and does the photo still represent? *Refer to the first sentence in this paragraph. What is the "whole story" that can be found in the legendary photo of Buzz Aldrin? Turn and talk. Accept reasonable answers based on text evidence.*

ⓨ 33. How can one photograph have so many possible meanings? *Depending on the viewer's perspective, one image can mean different and various things to different and various people.*

ⓩ 34. Why is this the most obvious? *It points out the huge gap between the capabilities of the first humans on Earth and the first humans on the moon.*

35. What is the literal meaning of how far the human race has come since its beginnings? *235,000 miles from Earth to the moon*

36. What is the figurative meaning of how far the human race has come since its beginnings? *Societal and technological advances, nations coming together rather than being isolated or unable to communicate, setting goals based on the impossible*

ⒶⒶ 37. What kinds of impossible things could people hope for? *Turn and talk, then share out. Elicit both technological and societal possibilities, such as: peace, cures for hunger and disease, and so on.*

ⒷⒷ 38. Which people would think this was the most important meaning? *Americans and nations who looked to the United States for peace and protection would interpret the picture of the American in a positive way, but other countries, especially the Soviets, might see America's accomplishment in a negative way.*

16

The Buzz Aldrin image we know as AS11-40-5903 will remain one of **CC**the most powerful existing representations of the achievements of humankind. Because of its **DD**bizarre beauty, its **EE**symbolic significance, and its widespread recognition as a **FF**major cultural marker, it will continue to **GG**inspire people to achieve great things, and it will **HH**long outlive the era in which it came to be.

CENTRAL IDEA:
Photographs are a powerful medium that capture more than a moment in time.

CC 39. Why is it such a powerful representation of man's achievements? *The space program achieved what people thought would be impossible. Unlike other great achievements of humankind, the moon landing was not on this Earth. The combination of the enticement of space and the bravery and determination of the astronauts makes the lunar landing greater than most. The photograph is powerful because it was able to capture that greatness as it happened.*

DD 40. What is its bizarre beauty? *The barren rock and darkness was a stark contrast to the astronaut's suit and the reflection of the spacecraft and the photographer. What might have seemed desolate under other circumstances seemed extraordinarily beautiful in this instance.*

EE 41. What is the symbolic significance? *The American triumph over the Soviets, the power of persistence, the reaching of unattainable goals, the hope for mankind*

FF 42. What is a *cultural marker? Elicit or define: It's like a bookmark in history: It marks an event that we remember, that causes change, or that represents the time period in which it happened.*

43. Why was it a major cultural marker? *It represented (or marked) the values and aspirations of U.S. society in the 1960s.*

GG 44. Why is the photo an inspiration? *It made everything (and anything) seem possible.*

HH 45. Why are photographs so powerful? *Turn and talk, then share out. Accept reasonable answers based on text evidence, including: They reflect unaltered truth, hold power over emotion, appeal to beliefs and desires, convey imaginative information.*

Man on the Moon:
ANNOTATED CONSTRUCTED RESPONSE EXEMPLAR

Recommended for Grades 5–7

Prompt: What does the author **really** want us to know about the power of a photograph?

Note: The following annotated exemplar is aligned with the Constructed Response Instructional Rubric Grades 5–8 (pages 158–159) and the Constructed Response Student Checklist Grades 5–8 (page 160).

The author wants us to know that even though a photograph captures a small moment in **Ⓐ**time, what the photo "says" is much more than that. "Photography is a powerful medium" because the camera catches a moment that becomes "frozen in time." Once we capture a moment with a camera, we can look at the picture, think about what happened, and remember it long after it's gone. This is powerful because the image in the photo may even change how we think long after it was taken. It may even become historically important to remember the time it was taken **Ⓑ**in.

Ⓐ Answer/Thesis

Ⓑ Text Evidence #1 Interwoven with Rationale

Ⓒ Text Evidence #2 Interwoven with Rationale

Ⓓ Text Evidence #3 Interwoven with Rationale

Ⓔ Conclusion Part A

Ⓕ Conclusion Part B

"Every photograph depicts a single moment of course, but in some of those single moments a whole story can be found." An example of this is the moon shot photo. It showed the astronaut in a space suit standing on the surface of the moon, but it told the story of the space race and the United States' triumph over the Soviet **Ⓒ**Union. Photos can also have "various possible meanings." Photo AS11-40-5903 meant victory to some Americans, and to others it represented hope. To the Soviets, the photo must have meant defeat, but to other countries it stood for unity. "One giant leap for mankind" was a statement about possibilities for everyone, not just for Americans. In a way, the picture of the man on the moon showed how far we had come from the beginning of humanity and an invitation for all to realize that even greater things were **Ⓓ**possible. The photo of Buzz Aldrin on the moon represents different things to different people, but what it represents most is the phenomenal, almost unbelievable trip to the moon made by three brave Americans. That in itself is a story for the ages, but even more amazing is that the picture had and still has the power to prove that there is no end to imagined possibilities for anyone and everyone in the **Ⓔ**world. The author writes that the Buzz Aldrin image "will remain one of the most powerful existing representations of the achievements of humankind." This famous photo makes us feel inspired to do great things, patriotic about our country, and amazed every time we look at **Ⓕ**it.

Tomb Explorers

by Nicola Barber

1 Imagine you are a farmer, digging away in a field. Suddenly, you spot something in the ground beneath your feet—a hole, a glint of metal, an underground chamber. It's a one in a million chance, but it can happen!

2 Some of the most incredible tomb discoveries have been made by chance, and some have unearthed dazzling treasures. Others, of course, are the result of painstaking research and careful archaeological work.

3 In past times, people were often buried with the things they would need in the afterlife. Even the poorest people were sometimes buried with a cooking pot or other everyday object. In the tombs of the wealthy or noble people, the objects considered necessary for the afterlife included: furniture, weapons, armor, jewelry, and even food.

4 Some places are difficult to explore on the ground. Lots of ancient remains are in hot deserts or in countries that are dangerous to visit. Using photographs taken from airplanes and satellite images, archaeologists can spot possible sites from marks and patterns on the ground that can only be seen from the sky. Of course, if they want to find out more, they still have to get to the site and explore further!

5 It is some time around 2000 BCE. On the banks of the Euphrates River, in the region called Mesopotamia, stands a city made of mud bricks. Its name is Ur. Around it is rich and fertile farmland, watered by the great river. Flash forward to modern times. All that is left of Ur are a few ruins, surrounded by the desert.

6 It was these ruins that brought British archaeologist Charles Leonard Woolley to Iraq in 1922. Woolley had permission to start excavations at the site of the ancient city. He and his team began digging in 1923. Little did they know that their work at the site was to continue for another 11 years …

7

Over the next few years, Woolley unearthed the remains of houses and everyday objects that told him about how the people of Ur (the Sumerians) lived. In 1926, Ur's "Royal Cemetery" was excavated, which revealed spectacular objects. These included a gold necklace decorated with precious stones, as well as a small wooden box beautifully decorated with shell and the blue gemstone lapis lazuli. Woolley and his team were amazed. They were sure these objects came from the tombs of kings and queens!

8

Meanwhile, excavation of the royal tombs in the Valley of the Kings in Egypt had become well known. A British archaeologist named Howard Carter was convinced that there was one tomb that lay undiscovered—and clues suggested it could be that of a little-known pharaoh named Tutankhamun.

9

Carter's work was being paid for by a wealthy sponsor, the fifth Earl of Carnarvon. However, after years of searching with no result, Lord Carnarvon was running out of money and patience.

10

Carter decided to excavate one small triangle of ground that was still unexplored. After only three days, he made an amazing discovery—steps leading down to a sealed tomb. Carter checked that the seals were intact, then he re-covered the steps and sent a telegram to Lord Carnarvon in England.

11

"At last have made wonderful discovery in valley. A magnificent tomb with seals intact. Re-covered same for your arrival. Congratulations."

12

Work on the excavation restarted when Lord Carnarvon arrived. The first doorway opened to a passage full of rubble. Carter and the others cleared the rubble away and came to a second doorway covered in Tutankhamun's seals. What would they find on the other side? A looted chamber, or a treasure trove? Carefully, Carter made a small hole in the corner and peered in by the light of a candle.

"As my eyes grew accustomed to the light, details of the room emerged slowly from the mist, strange animals, statues, and gold—everywhere the glint of gold. For the moment—an eternity it must have seemed to the others standing by—I was struck dumb with amazement, and when Lord Carnarvon, unable to stand in suspense any longer, inquired anxiously, 'Can you see anything?' It was all I could do to get out the words, 'Yes, wonderful things.'"

The room that Carter and Lord Carnarvon first glimpsed turned out to be an antechamber. It was filled with hundreds of objects that Tutankhamun was thought to need in the afterlife—beds, ointment jars, and games. Later, Carter finally opened the burial chamber. The ancient Egyptian boy-king, Tutankhamun, was buried in a gold sarcophagus, and his tomb contained his golden throne, chariot, and countless other amazing objects, untouched and unseen for 3,000 years.

The discovery of an ancient tomb does not just uncover gold and riches. It can also give us important information about people's lives in the distant past. Some of the most exciting recent finds have been in South America.

In 2011, archaeologists uncovered tomb sites in Peru that belonged to the Wari people. The Wari civilization flourished in the Andes mountains region between AD 600 and 1000. In the tombs were gold bracelets, a silver mask, and a silver chest plate as well as silver-coated walking sticks and small models of cats. The archaeologists now hope that future finds will tell them a lot more about these little-known people.

Around the world, there are many ancient tombs that still lie shrouded in mystery. We may never know what is inside them, or who they belonged to, or why they were made. But it is possible that future technology may reveal more about such mysterious sites.

Clearly, finding a tomb requires a lot of dedication. It can take years of research, and then years more of hard work on the ground, and even then you might never find anything. You need to be fit, brave, and able to endure harsh conditions. Most of all, you need to be lucky.

Tomb Explorers:
TEACHER DISCUSSION GUIDE

Grade Level: 5–8, Guided Reading Level: V, Lexile Level: 1050L

1

ⒶImagine you are a farmer, digging away in a field. Suddenly, you spot something in the ground beneath your feet—a hole, a glint of metal, an underground chamber. **Ⓑ**It's a one in a million chance, but it can happen!

2

Some of the most incredible tomb discoveries have been made by chance, and some have unearthed dazzling treasures. Others, of course, are the result of **Ⓒ**painstaking research and careful **Ⓓ**archaeological work.

3

In past times, people were often buried with the things they would need in the **Ⓔ**afterlife. Even the poorest people were sometimes buried with **Ⓕ**a cooking pot or other everyday object. In the tombs of the wealthy or noble people, the objects considered necessary for the afterlife included: **Ⓖ**furniture, weapons, armor, jewelry, and even food.

Ⓐ 1. Why did the author start with this kind of an introduction? *To engage the reader, to set a tone of intrigue, to simulate the excitement tomb explorers might feel upon discovering something of value*

Ⓑ 2. What is the author saying here? *It may be next to impossible to uncover a lost treasure by accident, but because there is a small chance and because it has happened, we should not dismiss the possibility.*

Ⓒ 3. What does *painstaking* mean? *Elicit from context clues: done with extreme care or thoroughness.*

Ⓓ 4. What is archaeological work? *Elicit or define: analysis of the material remains (artifacts) of the past to gain an understanding of human culture at that time.*

5. What is the author implying about archaeological work? *That it can be both thrilling and tedious, but rewarding still*

Ⓔ 6. What does this tell you about ancient beliefs? *People believed in life after death.*

Ⓕ 7. Why would poor people be buried with a cooking pot or everyday objects? *To be sure their basic needs (sustenance) would be met in the next world.*

8. What does this tell you about their beliefs? *They believed they would be human in the next life, they would need to eat, they would have to cook for themselves, they would live a similar life.*

Ⓖ 9. How did the things found in the tombs of wealthy people differ from those found in poorer people's tombs? *The wealthy had luxuries while the poor had everyday objects.*

10. What does this tell you about their beliefs? *The wealthy also thought their societal status would stay the same. They took luxuries rather than necessities, which implies they would have servants to cook their food. The need for weapons implies they would encounter conflicts in the afterlife, much like they did on Earth.*

4

Some places are difficult to explore on the ground. Lots of ancient remains are in hot deserts or in countries that are dangerous to visit. Using photographs taken from airplanes and satellite images, archaeologists can spot possible sites from marks and patterns on the ground that can only be seen from the sky. Of course, **❶**if they want to find out more, they still have to get to the site and explore further!

5

❶It is some time around 2000 BCE. **❶**On the banks of the Euphrates River, in the region called Mesopotamia, stands a city made of mud bricks. Its name is Ur. Around it is rich and fertile farmland, watered by the great river. **❶**Flash forward to modern times. **❶**All that is left of Ur are a few ruins, surrounded by the desert.

6

It was these ruins that brought British archaeologist Charles Leonard Woolley to **❶**Iraq in 1922. Woolley **❶**had permission to start excavations at the site of the ancient city. He and his team began digging in 1923. Little did they know that their work at the site was to continue for **❶**another 11 years …

7

Over the next few years, Woolley unearthed the remains of houses and everyday objects that told him about how the people of Ur (the Sumerians) lived. In 1926, Ur's "Royal Cemetery" was excavated, which revealed spectacular objects. These included a gold necklace decorated with precious stones, as well as a small wooden box beautifully decorated with shell and the blue gemstone lapis lazuli. Woolley and his team were amazed. They were sure these objects came from the tombs of **❶**kings and queens!

8

❶Meanwhile, excavation of the royal tombs in the Valley of the Kings in Egypt had become well known. A British archaeologist named Howard Carter was convinced that there was one tomb that lay undiscovered—and clues suggested it could be that of a little-known pharaoh named **❶**Tutankhamun.

❶ 11. What does this tell you about archaeologists? *Turn and talk, then share out. Elicit that they are brave, persistent, adventurous, curious.*

12. Why would they be willing to go into a desert or a dangerous country to explore a potential site? *The pull of discovery drives their exploration.*

❶ 13. What literary device is the author using here? *Flashback*

14. Why is it being used? *To help the reader visualize why ruins have to be excavated or dug up*

❶ 15. What visual impression of Ur does this create? *It's a large city built on the banks of a huge river surrounded by green, fertile farmland.*

❶ 16. Why does the author include this sentence? *To indicate the flashback is over and to move the reader back to modern day quickly*

17. What does the word *modern* mean in this context? *Modern in the sense that it is not ancient, 1922 (referenced in paragraph 6) indicates it does not mean present day*

❶ 18. How does this image differ from the ancient one? *The thriving city is gone, the river is gone, the farmland is gone. What's left is a barren desert.*

19. How does this help us understand why archaeologists have to dig up their findings? *The geography of the region changed from fertile to desert. We can infer that over thousands of years the desert sand covered the city.*

❶ 20. Why did Woolley go to Iraq? *Ancient Mesopotamia and Ur were located in what is now Iraq.*

❶ 21. Why did Woolley need permission? *To start the excavations in Iraq*

❶ 22. What does this imply? *It reinforces the idea that archaeology is a painstakingly slow process. It also implies that there was much to unearth, and the discovery was a great one.*

❶ 23. Why was Woolley sure the spectacular objects came from royal tombs? *They were very different from the everyday objects uncovered in the city of Ur, and they were so beautiful, even the archaeologists were amazed.*

❶ 24. What does *meanwhile* mean in this context? *At the same time; simultaneously*

25. How does the word *meanwhile* help readers understand the time sequence of the text? *The excavations in Iraq were going on at the same time as the excavations in Egypt.*

❶ 26. What does this tell you about Howard Carter? *He was a tomb explorer, he had a special interest in Tutankhamun, he was driven by the allure of a "one in a million chance."*

9

Carter's work was being paid for by a **S**wealthy sponsor, the fifth Earl of Carnarvon. However, after years of searching with no result, Lord Carnarvon was **T**running out of money and patience.

10

Carter decided to excavate one small triangle of ground that was still unexplored. **U**After only three days, he made an amazing discovery—steps leading down to a sealed tomb. Carter checked that the **V**seals were intact, then he **W**re-covered the steps and sent a **X**telegram to Lord Carnarvon in England.

11

Y"At last have made wonderful discovery in valley. A magnificent tomb with seals intact. Re-covered same for your arrival. Congratulations."

12

Work on the excavation restarted when Lord Carnarvon arrived. The first doorway opened to a passage **Z**full of rubble. Carter and the others cleared the rubble away and came to a second doorway covered in Tutankhamun's seals. What would they find on the other side? **AA**A looted chamber, or a treasure trove? **BB**Carefully, Carter made a small hole in the corner and peered in by the light of a candle.

S 27. What is a *sponsor? Discuss that it is someone who provides money to support a project or an endeavor.*

T 28. Why would Carnarvon be running out of money? *Carter's work was costly.*

29. Why would Carnarvon be running out of patience? *Carter had been searching for Tutankhamun for many years with no result.*

U 30. How does this equate to Carter's "one in a million chance"? *After so many years of nothing, in only three days of digging, he found what he was looking for.*

V 31. Why was this important? *If the seals were intact, the tomb had not been disturbed since the seals were put in place.*

W 32. What does *re-covered* mean in this context? *Cover again*

33. Why did he re-cover the steps? *He didn't want anyone else to find them before Carnarvon got there.*

X 34. What is a *telegram? A message sent by telegraph (signals sent over a wire) and then delivered in written or printed form. It was the fastest way of communication in 1922, but is no longer used.*

35. Why did he send the telegram? *To let his sponsor know that he had finally made a discovery.*

Y 36. Why does the language seem stilted? *Elicit or explain: Carter was trying to be as explicit as possible using the least number of words because the cost of a telegram was based on the number of words used.*

37. What does *same* refer to? *The magnificent tomb*

38. Why did Carter re-cover the steps to the tomb? *So that Carnarvon could participate in the excitement of the find. He was waiting for Carnarvon to get to Egypt before doing anything else.*

39. Why did Carter congratulate Carnarvon? *Carnarvon's financial support had made the find possible. Carter was appreciative of the support and congratulated Carnarvon as a way of thanking him for not giving up.*

Z 40. What does *rubble* mean in this context? *Rock or stone debris*

AA 41. What does *looted chamber* mean in this context? *A large room from which all of the valuables had been stolen*

42. What is a *treasure trove? Discovered hidden valuables*

43. Why was Carter unsure about what he would find on the other side? *He suspected he had found Tutankhamun's tomb, but couldn't be sure. He had been searching for so long, he didn't want to be overconfident; he was hoping this was his "one in a million chance."*

BB 44. Why was Carter being so careful? *He didn't want to damage anything and he didn't want anything to go wrong.*

13

CC "As my eyes grew accustomed to the light, details of the room emerged slowly from the mist, strange animals, statues, and gold—everywhere the glint of gold. For the moment—an eternity it must have seemed to the others standing by—I was struck dumb with amazement, and when Lord Carnarvon, unable to stand in suspense any longer, inquired anxiously, 'Can you see anything?' It was all I could do to get out the words, 'Yes, wonderful things.'"

14

The room that Carter and Lord Carnarvon first glimpsed turned out to be an DD antechamber. It was filled with hundreds of objects that Tutankhamun was thought to need in the afterlife—EE beds, ointment jars, and games. Later, Carter finally opened the burial chamber. The ancient Egyptian boy-king, Tutankhamun, was buried in a FF gold sarcophagus, and his tomb contained GG his golden throne, chariot, and countless other amazing objects, HH untouched and unseen for 3,000 years.

15

II The discovery of an ancient tomb does not just uncover gold and riches. It can also give us important information about people's lives in the distant past. Some of the most exciting recent finds have been in South America.

16

In 2011, archaeologists uncovered tomb sites in Peru that belonged to the Wari people. The Wari civilization flourished in the Andes mountains region between AD 600 and 1000. In the tombs were gold bracelets, a silver mask, and a silver chest plate as well as silver-coated walking sticks and small models of cats. The archaeologists now hope that future finds will tell them a lot more about these JJ little-known people.

CC 45. What was Carter's reaction to what he saw? *Turn and talk, then share out. Elicit that he was speechless, awestruck, overwhelmed by the magnificence and abundance of what he saw.*

DD 46. What is an *antechamber*? *Elicit from context clues: an outer chamber that came before the burial chamber.*

EE 47. How does Tutankhamun's preparation for the afterlife compare with other's mentioned in the text? *They seem meant for a younger person, maybe someone who was sick, but the number of things would indicate he was royal.*

FF 48. What is a *sarcophagus*? *Elicit from context clues: a coffin.*

GG 49. What does this tell you about the boy-king? *Turn and talk. Accept reasonable answers based on text evidence, such as: He was highly regarded, he was wealthy, he was important to the kingdom.*

HH 50. To be sure students understand how important this discovery was, reconcile the time element by establishing how long ago 3,000 years was (King Tut died in 1323 BCE). Why was it a bonus that the findings were untouched? *They were intact from 3,000 years before. They would not have to be pieced back together like ruins would. It was a treasure trove in the greatest sense.*

II 51. How does the tone change here? *It changes from exciting to serious.*

52. What point is the author making? *Archaeology is about the excitement of uncovering treasures, but more importantly, it's about the excitement of studying people's lives from the past so that we can make sense of our own.*

JJ 53. Why are we interested in studying ancient cultures? *Turn and talk. Accept reasonable answers based on text evidence. Elicit that with each new find, we are more informed about our past, and the potential for new finds is what drives the tomb explorers to continue their quests.*

17

Around the world, there are many ancient tombs that still lie shrouded in mystery. We may never know what is inside them, or who they belonged to, or why they were made. **K K** But it is possible that future technology may reveal more about such mysterious sites.

18

L L Clearly, finding a tomb requires a lot of dedication. It can take years of research, and then years more of hard work on the ground, and even then **M M** you might never find anything. You need to be fit, brave, and able to endure harsh conditions. Most of all, you need to be lucky.

K K 54. How does this add to the allure of discovery? *It reinforces the idea that we don't know all there is to know, and there is hope that the "one in a million chance" will become less about luck and more about careful archaeological work, yet still satisfy the excitement of the find.*

L L 55. Why is it clear that finding a tomb requires a lot of dedication? *The examples from Iraq and Egypt each took years to uncover or discover.*

M M 56. Why do archaeologists/tomb explorers continue to put so much time and dedication into their work knowing they might not ever find anything? *Turn and talk. Accept reasonable answers based on text evidence. Elicit that it is the thrill of the chase, the allure of the discovery that keeps them going. It is important to find the treasure troves, but it is equally exciting to find answers to questions we have about ancient cultures and the influence they have had on us.*

CENTRAL IDEA: The allure of discovery, of both treasures and information, drives archaeologists to dig deeply into the past.

Tomb Explorers:
ANNOTATED CONSTRUCTED RESPONSE EXEMPLAR
Recommended for Grades 5–8

Prompt: What does the author **really** want us to know about tomb explorers?

Note: The following annotated exemplar is aligned with the Constructed Response Instructional Rubric Grades 5–8 (pages 158–159) and the Constructed Response Student Checklist Grades 5–8 (page 160).

Ⓐ Answer/Thesis

Ⓑ Text Evidence #1 Interwoven with Rationale

Ⓒ Text Evidence #2 Interwoven with Rationale

Ⓓ Text Evidence #3 Interwoven with Rationale

Ⓔ Conclusion Part A

Ⓕ Conclusion Part B

Archaeologists are motivated by the allure of discovery and the potential to unearth treasure troves of both artifacts and information of past Ⓐcultures. According to the text, "some of the most incredible tomb discoveries have been made by chance" but others "are the result of painstaking research and careful archaeological work." Archaeologists spend many years of hard labor, often in difficult locations in the hope that they will find evidence of past cultures. It is clear that although some digs may yield spectacular finds, often their efforts may turn up little or nothing for many years, and yet, they still keep Ⓑdigging. "As my eyes grew accustomed to the light, details of the room emerged slowly from the mist, strange animals, statues, and gold—everywhere the glint of gold." These now-famous words of British archaeologist, Howard Carter, give us a glimpse into the first moments of one of the most spectacular, famous, and important archaeological finds ever, the tomb of Tutankhamun. Years of painstaking research and labor in the harsh climate of the desert had finally paid off. Although it was rare to find such spectacular remains, Carter and Lord Carnarvon were willing to spend vast amounts of money and time in the hopes that they might be Ⓒlucky. "The discovery of an ancient tomb does not just uncover gold and riches. It can also give us important information about people's lives in the distant past." The author explains throughout the text that in fact, the discovery of treasure troves of information of past cultures is the true goal of the archaeologist. The items that are found help us understand how the people lived their daily lives, what materials could be found in the area, and information about their culture and Ⓓbeliefs. The author wants us to understand the significance archaeology has in making connections between current and ancient cultures. "Around the world, there are many ancient tombs that still lie shrouded in mystery." The excitement of the hunt and the potential for discovery drives people in the field of archaeology to continue digging into the Ⓔpast. The text gives us a taste of the thrill of discovery that is part of this amazing field of science and gives us a sense of our place on the historical Ⓕtimeline.

Ethics of Sports

by Nick Hunter

1 You probably have an idea of what sportsmanship means to you. You might be able to think of an example from your favorite sport of someone showing great sportsmanship. You can probably also think of examples when an athlete showed bad sportsmanship. There are many examples of good and bad sportsmanship, as well as ethical questions that we all face in sports. But before we can consider these questions, we need to decide what we mean by "sportsmanship."

2 Sportsmanship is not just about following the rules of the game. Following the rules is a basic requirement for playing any sport, however, not all the rules of the game are exactly equal. Some are essential for the game to work, while others are less essential to making the game run smoothly. Although sportsmanship is not just about following the rules, the two can go together. A player who tries to get away with breaking rules may be guilty of bad sportsmanship.

3 Showing good sportsmanship, or being a good sport, is more about the spirit in which the game is played. A good sport can be contrasted with someone who tries to "win at all costs." Sportsmanship is about recognizing that playing the game fairly and in the right spirit is at least as important as winning. This does not mean that a good sport does not want to win. Rather, a good sport just wants to win fairly.

4 Some instances of sportsmanship are obvious examples of people doing the right thing. But there are also many cases that are not quite so clear. Because the rules of sportsmanship are not written down, what one person thinks is good or bad sportsmanship another might think is quite normal behavior.

5 Most athletes learn their first attitudes toward sportsmanship in school and after-school sports. This applies to top professionals as much as it does to anyone else. Surveys of school athletes in the United States have found that, while many students recognize the importance of sportsmanship, this is not universal. More than a third of boys and almost half of football players said it was more important to win than to be thought of as a good sport. Only 15 percent of girls thought that this was the case. Around 4 out of 10 boys and 3 out of 10 girls admitted that they had cheated or bent the rules at least once. The athletes were also asked specific questions, such as whether it was acceptable to fake an injury to gain their team a time-out. More than a third of boys and one in every five girls thought that this would be acceptable. Despite these figures, most students in the survey thought that fair play was an important part of sports.

Cleveland Stroud was coach of the Rockdale County High School basketball team in Conyers, Georgia. In 1967 the team won the Georgia boys championship for the first time, a great achievement for the school. After the trophy had been awarded, Stroud noticed that the school had accidentally allowed an ineligible player, who had not passed enough classes, to play in one of the team's games. (In many school sports, athletes have to pass a certain number of classes to be eligible for the sports team.) Stroud had no hesitation. A rule had been broken, and the trophy would have to be returned. Although this was difficult for all involved, the local community was immensely proud of the honesty the school had shown. "I told my team that people forget the scores of basketball games: they don't ever forget what you're made of." (High-school basketball coach, Cleveland Stroud)

One of the reasons why sportsmanship is important for all of us is because these skills transfer to our everyday lives. We all have to obey rules in life, whether they are about not cheating on tests or getting to school or work on time. We don't always have a referee checking when we do the right thing.

Sportsmanship is partly about following rules, but it is more about following principles. Sometimes these principles are tested in extreme conditions, but more often, these principles are tested in everyday situations—for example, when we have to decide whether it is right to lie about something or be disloyal to a friend. In life we have to deal with many of the same things we encounter in sports. Having a sense of sportsmanship helps us to deal with defeats and setbacks graciously. It also helps us to be modest about our successes, recognizing that they are rarely achieved without help from others. Having a sense of fair play and the importance of working on a team helps us build strong relationships off the sports field, just as they do on the field.

Ethics of Sports:
TEACHER DISCUSSION GUIDE

Grade Level: 6–8, Guided Reading Level: Z, Lexile Level: 1100L

1

You probably have an idea of what sportsmanship means to you. You might be able to think of an example from your favorite sport of someone showing great sportsmanship. You can probably also think of examples when an athlete showed bad sportsmanship. There are many examples of good and bad sportsmanship, as well as **Ⓐ**ethical questions that we all face in sports. But before we can consider these questions, we need to decide what we mean by **Ⓑ**"sportsmanship."

2

Sportsmanship is not just about following the rules of the game. Following the rules is a basic requirement for playing any sport, however, **Ⓒ**not all the rules of the game are exactly equal. Some are essential for the game to work, while others are less essential to making the game run smoothly. Although sportsmanship is not just about following the rules, the two can go together. **Ⓓ**A player who tries to get away with breaking rules may be guilty of bad sportsmanship.

3

Showing good sportsmanship, or being a good sport, is more about the **Ⓔ**spirit in which the game is played. A good sport can be contrasted with someone who tries to **Ⓕ**"win at all costs." Sportsmanship is about recognizing that playing the game fairly and in the right spirit is at least as important as winning. This does not mean that a good sport does not want to win. Rather, a good sport just wants to win fairly.

4

Some instances of sportsmanship are obvious examples of people doing the right thing. But there are also many cases that are **Ⓖ**not quite so clear. Because the rules of sportsmanship are not written down, what one person thinks is good or bad sportsmanship another might think is quite normal behavior.

Ⓐ 1. What are examples of ethical questions in sports? *Is it ethical to fake an injury or injure an opponent to gain an advantage for your team?*

Ⓑ 2. What does sportsmanship mean to you? *Turn and talk and share both good and bad examples. Accept reasonable answers.*

Ⓒ 3. Can you give examples of these two types of rules? *Accept reasonable answers, such as: In tennis, rules for order of the serve, boundary lines, and how a point is scored would be essential; whether or not a foot fault is called would be less essential.*

Ⓓ 4. How can you use an example from question 3 to explain this? *Example: A player's inadvertent foot fault that goes unnoticed would not be considered bad sportsmanship, but a deliberate step across the line when the line judge wasn't looking would be.*

5. Why would this be considered bad sportsmanship? *Breaking the rules is bad sportsmanship, whether or not you get caught, and just because you don't get caught doesn't make it OK to break rules. It is a matter of what is considered fair play and is influenced by the player's character.*

Ⓔ 6. What is the right spirit in which to play the game? *To want to win, but to want to win fairly by following the rules and treating teammates, opponents, and the referees with integrity and respect*

Ⓕ 7. What does it mean to *win at all costs? Turn and talk, then share. Elicit that it means caring more about winning than about how the game is played.*

8. How is winning at all costs different from winning fairly? *Turn and talk, then share. Accept reasonable answers based on text evidence.*

Ⓖ 9. Why are there cases that are *not quite so clear? Because the rules of sportsmanship aren't written down, they are open to interpretation. Different perspectives can bring about different interpretations of good and bad sportsmanship.*

5

Most athletes **H**learn their first attitudes toward sportsmanship in school and after-school sports. This applies to top professionals as much as it does to anyone else. Surveys of school athletes in the United States have found that, while many students recognize the importance of sportsmanship, **I**this is not universal. More than a third of boys and almost half of football players said **J**it was more important to win than to be thought of as a good sport. Only 15 percent of girls thought that this was the case. **K**Around 4 out of 10 boys and 3 out of 10 girls admitted that they had cheated or bent the rules at least once. The athletes were also asked specific questions, such as whether it was acceptable to fake an injury to gain their team a time-out. More than a third of boys and one in every five girls thought that this would be acceptable. Despite these figures, most students in the survey thought that fair play was an important part of sports.

6

Cleveland Stroud was coach of the Rockdale County High School basketball team in Conyers, Georgia. In 1967 the team won the Georgia boys championship for the first time, a great achievement for the school. After the trophy had been awarded, Stroud noticed that the school had accidentally allowed an ineligible player, who had not passed enough classes, to play in one of the team's games. (In many school sports, athletes have to pass a certain number of classes to be eligible for the sports team.) **L**Stroud had no hesitation. A rule had been broken, and the trophy would have to be returned. Although this was difficult for all involved, the local community was **M**immensely proud of the honesty the school had shown. "I told my team that people forget the scores of basketball games: they don't ever forget **N**what you're made of." (High-school basketball coach, Cleveland Stroud)

7

One of the reasons why sportsmanship is important for all of us is because these skills **O**transfer to our everyday lives. We all have to **P**obey rules in life, whether they are about not cheating on tests or getting to school or work on time. We don't always **Q**have a referee checking when we do the right thing.

H 10. How do different interpretations of good and bad sportsmanship affect what young athletes are taught? *Students can learn different attitudes from different instructors, which sends mixed messages about what good sportsmanship is.*

I 11. What does this mean? *Elicit from context clues that not everyone felt the same about the importance of sportsmanship.*

J 12. What is the contradiction the author is presenting? *Student responses demonstrate the result of being sent those mixed messages. They admit they have cheated, yet support fair play.*

K 13. What does this data say about student understanding of good sportsmanship? *They are mixing the ethics of gamesmanship (winning at all costs) and the ethics of sportsmanship (winning through fair play) based on what they have been taught. Coaches are sending mixed or different messages to their players depending on their personal beliefs, which causes ethical questions to arise and leaves students confused about how they should conduct themselves during competition.*

L 14. Why didn't he hesitate? *His personal rules of sportsmanship prevented him from keeping something his team didn't deserve. He was sending a clear, not a mixed, message to his players, the school, and the community, and he was demonstrating good sportsmanship in doing so.*

M 15. Why was the community *immensely proud* of the school's honesty? *Doing the right thing takes courage, and the community appreciated the integrity of the coach and the example he set for all who were affected by his decision.*

N 16. What does this phrase mean? *It is an idiom that refers to one's moral fiber—the essence of one's character.*

17. What message was the coach sending to his team with this quote? *Good sportsmanship reflects good character, and it is more important to be remembered for your character than for how many points you scored in the basketball games.*

O 18. What does *transfer* mean in this context? *To be able to apply the rules of sportsmanship to situations both on and off the field*

P 19. What kind of rules is the author referring to? *Turn and talk. Have students share out and elicit that the rules in life are those that are set by school, family, and society.*

Q 20. What does the author mean by this? *The life rules he refers to are set in place to be followed always. This is an analogy to the playing field—good sportsmanship on the field and in life should be evident whether or not a referee is there to blow his whistle and remind us to do the right thing.*

21. Who are the *referees* in real life? *Parents, teachers, police officers, etc.*

8

Sportsmanship is partly about following rules, but **R**it is more about following principles. Sometimes these principles are tested in extreme conditions, but more often, these principles are tested in everyday situations—for example, when we have to decide whether it is right to **S**lie about something or be disloyal to a friend. In life we have to deal with many of the same things we encounter in sports. Having a sense of sportsmanship helps us to deal with **T**defeats and setbacks graciously. It also helps us to **U**be modest about our successes, recognizing that they are rarely achieved without help from others. Having a sense of fair play and the importance of working on a team **V**helps us build strong relationships off the sports field, just as they do on the field.

R 22. What are principles? *Elicit or provide the definition: beliefs that govern one's personal behavior; morals—knowing the difference between right and wrong.*

S 23. What are some other examples of everyday situations that test our principles? *Turn and talk, then share out. Be sure student examples incorporate character-building moral dilemmas rather than situations that are simply about following rules.*

T 24. Can you think of an example of someone handling a defeat or a setback graciously? *Have students give personal examples or reference Coach Stroud as an example.*

U 25. What does it mean to be modest about a success? *Use context clues to elicit: to be proud about your accomplishments without bragging or taking full credit for them knowing many people helped and supported you along the way.*

26. How is this related to sports and to life? *Sports: You may be the star of the team, but that doesn't mean you became the star without help from your teammates. Life: Politicians need help from constituents, singers need help from musicians, scholars need help from their teachers, etc.*

27. How would having this quality show what you're made of? *It shows integrity and fairness—two qualities of good character.*

V 28. Why is it important to build strong relationships off the sports field? *We interact with people all the time—at home, in school, at work—and the more positively we learn to get along, the bigger the "winners" we'll be in life.*

CENTRAL IDEA: Sportsmanship skills build character and reflect the principles by which we should all live our lives.

Ethics of Sports:
ANNOTATED CONSTRUCTED RESPONSE EXEMPLAR

Recommended for Grades 6–8

Prompt: What does the author **really** want us to know about sportsmanship?

Note: The following annotated exemplar is aligned with the Constructed Response Instructional Rubric Grades 5–8 (pages 158–159) and the Constructed Response Student Checklist Grades 5–8 (page 160).

Ⓐ Answer/Thesis

Ⓑ Text Evidence #1 Interwoven with Rationale

Ⓒ Text Evidence #2 Interwoven with Rationale

Ⓓ Text Evidence #3 Interwoven with Rationale

Ⓔ Conclusion Part A

Ⓕ Conclusion Part B

The author wants us to know that the rules of sportsmanship should be followed the same way the rest of the rules in our lives are **Ⓐ**followed. He points out that although there are no clear definitions of sportsmanship, there are rules for each sport that follow the "spirit of the game" and are similar to moral behavior in everyday life. An example showing both good sportsmanship and adherence to a personal set of standards is the case of Coach Cleveland Stroud. The coach decided that his team should give up its trophy because the team broke one of the rules. "Stroud had no hesitation. A rule had been broken, and the trophy would have to be returned." The rules of the game were intact, and clearly so were the personal principles of this inspirational **Ⓑ**coach. Although data in the text suggests that many students think it is all right to bend the rules, they also report that they believe that "fair play was an important part of sports." This moral dilemma is faced by both athletes and people in everyday situations. As the text states, "we don't always have a referee checking when we do the right thing," so we had better know right from wrong and act **Ⓒ**accordingly. The author also claims that sportsmanship-like behavior should positively influence people's lives. "Having a sense of sportsmanship helps us to deal with defeats and setbacks **Ⓓ**graciously." The intended message is that principled behavior, both on and off the sports field, can be learned and ultimately shows what we are "made **Ⓔ**of." Consequently, sportsmanship can help us become the best that we can be where it matters the most—in our daily lives with our friends, families, and **Ⓕ**communities.

Ethics of Politics

by Jilly Hunt

1 Politics is the way a country, state, or community is run, as well as the way it builds relationships with other governments or communities. The term *politics* comes from the Greek word *polis*, which means "city" or "state."

2 Leaders are always a part of politics. Different leaders have their own personal styles of leadership, but the way they lead their people usually fits within a certain political system. A political system is the general behavior of a government and the legal institutions it uses. Examples of political systems include democracy, monarchy, dictatorships, and communism.

3 Each type of political system operates in a different way and is based on a different set of beliefs. For example, democracy is government decided by the people. In a democracy, the candidate with the most votes usually wins the election. In some democracies the party with the most winning candidates forms the ruling government. In a monarchy, the rule of a country is passed down through a family, with leaders such as kings and queens. In a dictatorship, just one person rules the government. Some political systems are defined by their economic practices. For example, in the system of communism, the state controls every aspect of the economy.

4 What are ethics? Ethics are concerned with what is good or bad, right or wrong. The term *ethics* is also used to describe a person's or government's moral values or principles. Ethics are about how people live their lives. The ethics of politics examines the way a country is run.

5 Ideas about ethics can be complicated, with people holding different beliefs. So, who is to judge? If not everyone agrees on the same moral principles, who decides whether a person or government has behaved ethically? For example, leaders of a country have to make some difficult decisions such as whether to go to war, knowing that hundreds or thousands of people may lose their homes or be killed. War presents leaders with many ethical decisions to make.

6 The personality of a leader will vary from individual to individual, but successful leaders often have similar traits. An ability to communicate is an essential part of successful leadership.

7

U.S. president John F. Kennedy was quiet and shy as a child, yet he is now considered one of the most popular presidents of modern times. He used the media to great effect to communicate with the voters of the United States. He had style and charisma, and together with his wife, Jacqueline, he promoted U.S. culture around the world. U.S. president Franklin D. Roosevelt showed his great ability to communicate, as he told the people of America in a fireside chat about the need for backing Britain in World War II even though this might take the country into war.

8

The power of personality is not always a good thing, however. German leader Adolf Hitler is thought of today as evil in human form, but he had a strong ability to persuade people. Hitler created a cult of personality around himself, meaning he created a sense of devotion among the people who followed him. Posters and other forms of communication promoted Hitler and made him a symbol of strength and virtue. People would greet each other by saying "Heil Hitler" and performing a Nazi salute. Children were encouraged to report adults they encountered whose views did not agree with the Nazi ideals. Was Hitler educating the German people or brainwashing them? Is it ethical to "educate" or train people into thinking a certain way?

9

Leadership can also be about working for the good of others. The U.S. civil rights leader Martin Luther King Jr. became a leader of the African American community because of his position as a church leader, but also because of his values. He encouraged his followers to take the high moral ground and not to sink to the level of violence that their opponents showed.

10

Nelson Mandela, the first black president of South Africa, is admired because of his ability to forgive those who imprisoned him for so many years. Instead of seeking revenge on the group that oppressed him, Mandela worked to achieve peace in the country that he loves.

11

"Politics is a jungle: torn between doing the right thing and staying in office—between local interest and national interest—between the private good of the politician and the general good." (John F. Kennedy) This quote from John F. Kennedy sums up the difficulties a leader faces while in office. The world of politics is a complicated one. There are many different leaders who may all have a different set of beliefs that leads them to make different ethical decisions. It is easier to judge the past actions of a leader when we can see the whole picture of an event. It is much harder for the leader at the time to know how actions will interact with those of others to shape history.

Ethics of Politics:
TEACHER DISCUSSION GUIDE

Grade Level: 6–8, Guided Reading Level: Y, Lexile Level: 1060L

1

ⒶPolitics is the way a country, state, or community is run, as well as Ⓑthe way it builds relationships with other governments or communities. The term *politics* comes from the Greek word *polis*, which means "city" or "state."

2

ⒸLeaders are always a part of politics. ⒹDifferent leaders have their own personal styles of leadership, but Ⓔthe way they lead their people usually fits within a certain political system. A political system is the general behavior of a government and the legal institutions it uses. Examples of political systems include democracy, monarchy, dictatorships, and communism.

3

ⒻEach type of political system operates in a different way and is based on a different set of beliefs. For example, democracy is government decided by the people. In a democracy, the candidate with the most votes usually wins the election. In some democracies the party with the most winning candidates forms the ruling government. In a monarchy, the rule of a country is passed down through a family, with leaders such as kings and queens. In a dictatorship, just one person rules the government. Some political systems are defined by their economic practices. For example, in the system of communism, the state controls every aspect of the economy.

Ⓐ 1. What is *politics? Twofold: the way a country, state, or community is run; and the way it builds relationships with other governments or communities*

Ⓑ 2. Why is it important for governments to build relationships with other governments? *Turn and talk. Accept reasonable answers based on text evidence, such as: Those of like beliefs can band together to gain strength and/or advantage, relationships can be used to influence decisions, opposing governments can negotiate if they have established relationships.*

Ⓒ 3. What is a *leader? Elicit from context clues: a person who leads or directs and is responsible for a group of people.*

Ⓓ 4. What would determine a leader's *personal style of leadership? Personality, personal interactions, experience, background, culture, etc.*

Ⓔ 5. What is a *political system? The structure of the government and how its laws and judicial system function*

6. What is a *legal institution? The laws and judicial system used by a government*

7. What are some examples of political systems? *Democracy, monarchy, dictatorships, communism*

8. How is the way a leader leads different from a personal style of leadership? *The way he or she leads is determined by the political system, the personal style of leadership is determined by the leader's personality.*

Ⓕ 9. What are the major differences among the four different political systems listed? *Turn and talk. Accept reasonable answers based on text evidence.*

10. What is a *set of beliefs? The standards that determine how a country is run. The set of beliefs is based on values, principles, and morals.*

11. How can a set of beliefs influence the way a political system operates? *Turn and talk. Accept reasonable answers, such as: It determines how ethical decisions are made, what rules people need to follow, punishment, civil rights, etc.*

4

G What are ethics? Ethics are concerned with what is good or bad, right or wrong. The term *ethics* is also used to describe a person's or government's moral values or principles. Ethics are about how people live their lives. The ethics of politics examines the way a country is run.

5

H Ideas about ethics can be complicated, with people holding different beliefs. **I** So, who is to judge? If not everyone agrees on the same moral principles, who decides whether a person or government has behaved ethically? For example, **J** leaders of a country have to make some difficult decisions such as whether to go to war, knowing that hundreds or thousands of people may lose their homes or be killed. **K** War presents leaders with many ethical decisions to make.

6

L The personality of a leader will vary from individual to individual, but successful leaders often have similar traits. **M** An ability to communicate is an essential part of successful leadership.

G 12. What are *ethics? Elicit or define: Ethics relate to actions and decisions. Ethical behavior is determined by the set of societal or political beliefs within a country, state, or community.*

13. How do ethics affect the way people live their lives? *Ethical people know the difference between right and wrong, so they live their lives in a way that matches the belief system of their culture.*

14. How are the ethics of politics different from personal ethics? *The ethics of politics are based on the political system of a country and affect the behavior of the government toward its people and toward other governments and cultures. Personal ethics are determined by the individual and affect the way a person lives his or her life.*

H 15. Why are ethics complicated? *If groups of people have different beliefs, the definition of right and wrong may be different for each group.*

I 16. Who *is* to judge? *Turn and talk. Elicit that there is no definitive answer because of the many differences in belief systems around the world.*

J 17. Why is going to war a difficult decision to make? *Killing people is considered unethical by most people in the world.*

K 18. What kinds of ethical decisions do leaders have to make when their countries are at war? *Turn and talk. Accept reasonable answers based on text evidence.*

L 19. What is a *personality? Elicit or define: the combined set of characteristics, attributes, and mannerisms that make each individual unique*

20. What kind of traits is the author referring to? *A specific quality or ability exhibited by an individual*

21. How can leaders have different personalities yet share similar traits? *Personality is determined by all of the qualities a person possesses. A single trait is just one part of a person's personality. People can share similar traits yet show very different personalities.*

M 22. What does *essential* mean? *Elicit from context clues: absolutely necessary, extremely important.*

23. What trait does the author say is essential for successful leadership? *An ability to communicate*

24. What can you infer about successful leaders? *They have the ability to communicate well.*

7

N U.S. president John F. Kennedy was quiet and shy as a child, yet he is now considered one of the most popular presidents of modern times. He used the media to great effect to communicate with the voters of the United States. He had style and charisma, and together with his wife, Jacqueline, he promoted U.S. culture around the world. **O** U.S. president Franklin D. Roosevelt showed his great ability to communicate, as he told the people of America in a fireside chat about the need for backing Britain in World War II even though this might take the country into war.

8

P The power of personality is not always a good thing, however. German leader **Q** Adolf Hitler is thought of today as evil in human form, but he had a strong ability to persuade people. **R** Hitler created a cult of personality around himself, meaning he created a sense of devotion among the people who followed him. **S** Posters and other forms of communication promoted Hitler and made him a symbol of strength and virtue. People would greet each other by saying "Heil Hitler" and performing a Nazi salute. Children were encouraged to report adults they encountered whose views did not agree with the Nazi ideals. Was Hitler educating the German people or brainwashing them? **T** Is it ethical to "educate" or train people into thinking a certain way?

N 25. How did President Kennedy become so popular? *He was very charismatic and used that quality and the help of the media to connect with the people of the United States.*

26. How did JFK use his traits of style and charisma to communicate? *He traveled around the world promoting the United States, and the result was that he inspired others to like him, and consequently the United States.*

O 27. What is a *fireside chat? Elicit or define: an informal address over radio or television made famous by FDR.*

P 28. What is the *power of personality? The ability of a person to use his or her personality to gain power over others*

29. Why is the power of a personality not always a good thing? *If a person uses his or her powerful personality in a negative way, it can have a negative effect on the people he or she influences.*

Q 30. Who was Adolf Hitler? *Elicit or explain: He was chancellor of Germany from 1933 to 1945 and dictator of Nazi Germany from 1934 to 1945. Provide enough information for students to understand why the power of his personality was not a good thing, and why the author referred to him as "evil in human form" without losing sight of the path of the discussion and the specified central idea of the text.*

R 31. How did Hitler create a *cult of personality around himself? He used his strong ability to persuade people and the media to create a sense of devotion among the people who followed him. That devotion was extreme: "Heil Hitler" greetings, salutes, and the pressure on everyone to agree with the Nazi ideals.*

S 32. How did Hitler get people to follow him? *Turn and talk. Elicit specific details from the text, including: media promoted him, he became a symbol, people saluted him, children tattled on adults who weren't following him. He also had a strong ability to persuade people.*

33. How does Hitler's powerful personality seem different from JFK's and FDR's? *Hitler promoted himself in a way that ended up hurting people. JFK and FDR promoted themselves for the good of society.*

T 34. Ask the question, then have students turn and talk. *Elicit that it depends upon the message of the teaching or training. If its purpose is ethical (right or good), then the training would be considered ethical. If the purpose is unethical (as it was with Hitler), then the training would be considered unethical.*

9

U Leadership can also be about working for the good of others. The U.S. civil rights leader Martin Luther King Jr. became a leader of the African American community because of his position as a church leader, but also because of his values. He encouraged his followers to take the high moral ground and not to sink to the level of violence that their opponents showed.

10

V Nelson Mandela, the first black president of South Africa, is admired because of his ability to forgive those who imprisoned him for so many years. Instead of seeking revenge on the group that oppressed him, Mandela worked to achieve peace in the country that he loves.

U 35. How did MLK use his personal beliefs to lead the African American community? *He led by example. He had strong values that he used to encourage his followers to gain their civil rights by doing the right thing—avoiding the violence and negative behavior shown by their opponents.*

36. What does the author mean by *the high moral ground? Refusing to act in ways that are not viewed as ethical or morally right*

37. How did MLK work for the good of others? *He helped people get what they wanted by teaching them to be ethical in their methods.*

V 38. What did Nelson Mandela forgive? *Many years of imprisonment and oppression (prolonged cruel and unjust treatment)*

39. How does Nelson Mandela's leadership style mirror MLK's? *He too took the high moral ground to accomplish his goals. He wanted peace in his country, so he chose forgiveness over revenge to reach his ultimate goal.*

11

Ⓦ "Politics is a jungle: Ⓧ torn between doing the right thing and staying in office—between local interest and national interest—between the private good of the politician and the general good." (John F. Kennedy) This quote from John F. Kennedy sums up the difficulties a leader faces while in office. Ⓨ The world of politics is a complicated one. Ⓩ There are many different leaders who may all have a different set of beliefs that leads them to make different ethical decisions. ⒶⒶ It is easier to judge the past actions of a leader when we can see the whole picture of an event. ⒷⒷ It is much harder for the leader at the time to know how actions will interact with those of others to shape history.

CENTRAL IDEA: A leader makes ethical decisions using a combination of personal and political beliefs, what he or she knows about the beliefs of others, and what seems to be the best course of action at the time.

Ⓦ 40. Why did JFK use this metaphor? *He was comparing the competition to survive in politics to the competition to survive in the jungle. This references power (successful predators), competition (for food, dominance), and obtaining scarce resources (dog-eat-dog mentality).*

41. What does the metaphor mean? *Politics is a difficult thing to be involved in.*

Ⓧ 42. What do these comparisons explain about the difficulty leaders have due to politics? *Turn and talk. Elicit that there is a constant conflict between the self-interest of the leader and the unselfish interest in the common good. JFK is saying that a politician has to constantly be aware of the dangers of the "jungle" and how he will survive long enough to do something for the good of the country.*

Ⓨ 43. Why is politics so complicated? *There are many leaders who may all have a different set of beliefs that leads them to make different ethical decisions.*

Ⓩ 44. How do the leaders decide what is ethical and what isn't? *They have to look at the factors and possible outcomes, and then decide what's best for everyone in the situation based on the set of beliefs governing the political system.*

45. What is a trait that seems important for a successful leader to possess? *High moral values and principles—ethical beliefs and behaviors*

ⒶⒶ 46. Why is it easier to judge the past than the present? *When we look back at something that has already happened, we can see all of the factors that contributed to the outcome. It's harder to judge decisions made in the present because often the contributing factors are not as obvious, and the long-term effects/outcomes are not yet known.*

ⒷⒷ 47. How does this explain the difficulties a leader has when faced with making ethical decisions? *Turn and talk. Elicit that making decisions while in a conflict is difficult because it is impossible to see and understand all of the possible outcomes involved. Ethical decisions are difficult because of the many different factors and perspectives a leader must consider. A leader can anticipate the effects of his or her actions, but only after a decision has been made is he or she able to measure its impact. A leader does the best that he or she can under the circumstances, calling on both political and personal ethics to guide decisions.*

48. What can you conclude about the connection between ethics and leadership? *Turn and talk. Elicit the central idea: It is a combination of knowledge, anticipation of outcomes, concern for the greater good, and personal and political ethics that guide ethical decisions. Leaders must take all of these things into consideration to make decisions that affect countries, societies, communities, and history.*

Ethics of Politics:
ANNOTATED CONSTRUCTED RESPONSE EXEMPLAR

Recommended for Grades 6–8

Prompt: What does the author **really** want us to know about the connection between ethics and leadership?

Note: The following annotated exemplar is aligned with the Constructed Response Instructional Rubric Grades 5–8 (pages 158–159) and the Constructed Response Student Checklist Grades 5–8 (page 160).

The author wants us to know that leaders have to consider their own personal and political beliefs and the beliefs of others when making ethical **Ⓐ**decisions. According to the text, "ethics are concerned with what is good or bad, right or wrong." Making a decision about right and wrong should be easy, but it can actually be very complicated because values and beliefs vary from country to country and even between people in the same country. "So, who is to judge? If not everyone agrees on the same moral principles, who decides whether a person or government has behaved ethically?" How does a leader decide whether or not to go to war, "knowing that hundreds or thousands of people may lose their homes or be killed"? Leaders considering whether to fight each other don't share the same beliefs (or they wouldn't be fighting), yet each one thinks he is "right." In order to make a decision about going to war, each leader must think about what's "right" for himself, his country, and his **Ⓑ**countrymen. Ethical leadership is "about working for the good of others." The author also wants us to know that "an ability to communicate is an essential part of successful leadership." Leaders often use this trait to convince the public that their decisions are good ones. Leaders like John F. Kennedy, Franklin D. Roosevelt, Martin Luther King Jr., and Nelson Mandela all used their leadership and powers of persuasion to influence people to support thoughts and actions that would benefit the common good. They encouraged people to "take the high moral ground" and to support them in their efforts to do the **Ⓒ**same. Leadership is also linked to politics. "Each type of political system operates in a different way and is based on a different set of beliefs." This makes ethics in government complicated because of the different beliefs and attitudes among different countries, states, and communities. Additionally, leaders must often consider how conflicting ideas among the public affect the collective good of the people. Sometimes what seems popular or important to a specific group is not what is best for the country. Ethical decision-making is a balancing act of values, morals, and principles that leaders must juggle to achieve acceptable **Ⓓ**results. "Politics is a jungle: torn between doing the right thing and staying in office—between local interest and national interest—between the private good of the politician and the general good." The author is saying that ethical decision-making by leaders is a difficult process in which they must consider many things. Successful leaders must decide what's best for the time, the situation, and the people involved, and try to make their decisions for all the right **Ⓔ**reasons. Leaders are remembered for the political and ethical decisions they make and are eventually judged by the results of those decisions. Successful leaders benefit from being ethical and thoughtful about their decisions before deciding to make **Ⓕ**them.

Ⓐ Answer/Thesis

Ⓑ Text Evidence #1 Interwoven with Rationale

Ⓒ Text Evidence #2 Interwoven with Rationale

Ⓓ Text Evidence #3 Interwoven with Rationale

Ⓔ Conclusion Part A

Ⓕ Conclusion Part B

APPENDIX

TABLE OF CONTENTS

THOUGHT CAPTURER
Purpose and Explanation

The Thought Capturer was designed to capture key points of the discussion for transition into writing. By capturing ideas in the structure of the organizer, students can synthesize and reflect on the discussion and organize those reflections in a way that prepares them for the structure of the written constructed response. As an example, compare the *Humpback Whales* Thought Capturer Exemplar on page 148 to the *Humpback Whales* Annotated Constructed Response Exemplar on page 149. Not only does the Thought Capturer push synthesis of ideas by purposefully eliciting rationale for the text evidence, it also pushes synthesis of a new idea so that it emerges naturally as a logical extension of the thinking involved during the close reading of the text.

It is recommended that a thorough explanation of the purpose for this piece is introduced through teacher modeling before students are asked to use it on their own. Practice with this tool should also be scaffolded so that students learn to use it in a way that teaches them to think. This is a key piece of the lesson in that it captures the shared thought of the discussion in the students' own words. The Thought Capturer promotes synthesis by asking students to transfer thoughts from the whole group into individual thoughts of their own. The transfer from oral to written discourse is difficult for most students. Use of the Thought Capturer as a vehicle to make that transfer creates a prewriting organizer that captures the deep thinking of the discussion. Students can use the power of shared thought as an impetus to express their own thoughts on paper.

Following is an explanation of each part of the Thought Capturer along with suggestions for its effective use as a tool for cognitive follow-through from the discussion. General directions for use with any discussion are included along with specific examples referenced on the *Humpback Whales* Thought Capturer Exemplar (page 148) and the *Humpback Whales* Annotated Constructed Response Exemplar (page 149).

Part 1

The **question** is the prompt for the written response and comes directly from the central idea elicited from the discussion. Use the prompt included with the Annotated Constructed Response Exemplar for each lesson to fill in the blank and complete the question at the top of the Thought Capturer in section 1.

For example, the central idea of Lesson 6: *Humpback Whales* (see Teacher Discussion Guide, page 89) is: *Humpback whales have human qualities and should be treated more "human(e)ly."* The prompt on the *Humpback Whales* Thought Capturer Exemplar is: *What does the author* really *want us to know about humpback whales?* "Humpback whales" was used to fill in the blank and complete the question at the top of the Thought Capturer in section 1.

The word *really* is in italics to emphasize the deep thinking students have done about the text. Because the specified central idea is inferential, students are being asked to move beyond a basic comprehension level to a level of understanding that is based on deep, thorough, critical thinking.

Central idea/thesis is included to help with the transition from reading-thinking to writing-thinking. Because the prompt is based on the central idea, the answer to the prompt must contain the central idea. For grades 5–8, the central idea is connected to the answer/thesis students will develop for their constructed responses. For grades 3–4, the answer/central idea is used to match the language of the constructed response rubric. (See Constructed Response Instructional Rubrics and Student Checklists Purpose and Explanation, page 152 and Thought Capturer, page 150.)

For example, the central idea on the *Humpback Whales* Thought Capturer Exemplar (page 148): *That they act like humans (they have human qualities), and they are intelligent, so we should think about treating them less like animals and more like us,* is applied in the thesis sentence of the *Humpback Whales* Annotated Constructed Response Exemplar (page 149) as: *The author wants us to know that we share many human-like qualities with humpback whales and that these very qualities should make us think about treating them more humanely.*

Part 2

Students are asked to be thoughtful about the **text evidence** they choose by selecting quotes that **most strongly** support the central idea and their thesis. This, too, connects the reading-thinking to the writing-thinking by turning students back to the text to evaluate evidence supporting the author's point of view (the central idea) at the same time they are gathering evidence to support their own answer or thesis. Looking for strong text evidence teaches students to choose evidence with a clear connection to their thesis and a logical connection to their reasoning.

For example, to support the answer/thesis that humpback whales have human qualities, the *Humpback Whales* Thought Capturer Exemplar (page 148) lists text evidence that clearly reflects human behavior. The first piece of evidence includes "communicate with each other." That by itself shows the human quality of communicating, but many animals communicate with each other. The addition of "and try to talk to us" makes the evidence more compelling and consequently more strongly supports the central idea that humpback whales are a different kind of animal—they're more human-like than we realize.

Introduce the words **rationale** and **relevant** together so that students gain a clear understanding of the purpose of each. When choosing text evidence to answer a question about the author's point of view, students need to include a rationale—an explanation—to validate their reason for choosing it. By introducing the word **relevant** at the same time, students learn to choose text evidence more prudently in order to be able to provide rationale to justify its selection.

For example, on the *Humpback Whales* Thought Capturer Exemplar (page 148), the text evidence "brain deeply folded similar to human brain" shows a strong physical similarity between the two animals but does not do much more than state a fact. Explaining the relevance of that fact provides an opportunity to push thinking through logical deductive reasoning. "Spindle cells in the brain affect language and emotion—same brain, same capabilities" is an inferential deduction made in the *Humpback Whales* Thought Capturer Exemplar as a result of having to explain the relevance of the evidence choice. That deduction became part of the argument supporting the thesis in the *Humpback Whales* Annotated Constructed Response Exemplar (page 149): *If the structure of a humpback's brain is similar to a human brain, perhaps humpback whales are capable of thinking similarly to humans.*

Part 3

The sequential logic of the Thought Capturer follows the sequential logic of the constructed response:
- Section 1: State the central idea (answer or thesis).
- Section 2: Find text evidence that strongly supports the central idea (answer or thesis) and explain why the text evidence supports the central idea (thesis) by providing rationale for its selection.
- Sections 3 and 4: Combine the individual rationales into a synthesized statement about the central idea to conclude.

For example, on the *Humpback Whales* Thought Capturer Exemplar (page 148), the text evidence rationale in section 2 points out the following:
- Whales are intelligent and a lot like humans.
- Because humpback whale brains and human brains are so similar in structure, they must have some of the same capabilities.
- Humpback whales are taught things rather than knowing what to do by instinct, which is a trait almost uniquely human.

The logical deduction, or synthesis, of the rationale stated in section 3 of the *Humpback Whales* Thought Capturer Exemplar is that whales are highly intelligent, and they clearly exhibit human qualities. This connects to the thesis by pointing out that not only do humpbacks act like humans, but they stand apart from other animals by doing so (from the *Humpback Whales* Annotated Constructed Response Exemplar, page 149), *which is different than most animals.*

Part 4

The **takeaway** is not a new idea from the students' heads. It is a new idea that evolves from the close reading and deep analysis of what the author is saying in the text. It should be a natural result of the synthesis that occurs when using the Thought Capturer, and should demonstrate a deep understanding of both the text and the discussion.

For example: The central idea from the *Humpback Whales* Thought Capturer Exemplar (page 148) suggests that we should think about treating the human-like humpback whales more humanely. The takeaway shown in section 4 of the exemplar is to use "OUR intelligence to realize" we should stop killing humpback whales. This idea transfers to the *Humpback Whales* Annotated Constructed Response Exemplar with a bit of irony: *Maybe a sign of human intelligence ...* proposing the question of who's the smarter animal.

Humpback Whales:
THOUGHT CAPTURER EXEMPLAR

1

What does the author *really* want us to know about ___humpback whales___ ?
(answer/thesis)

That they act like humans (they have human qualities), and they are intelligent,

so we should think about treating them less like animals and more like us

2

Which text evidence **most strongly** supports this answer/thesis?

Text Evidence	This is relevant because . . . (rationale)
• "doing some clever things" "communicate with each other" and try to talk to us • "brain deeply folded similar to human brain" • capable of learning and working together collaboratively rather than just using instinct like other (less intelligent) animals do	• Humpback whales don't just make noise—they have a language. That shows intelligence, and that they're like humans. • Spindle cells in the brain affect language and emotion—same brain, same capabilities. • There is evidence of higher-order thinking skills (many similar traits and behaviors; learning is a human thing).

3

How does your rationale connect to the answer/thesis? (Conclusion Part A)

The humpbacks exhibit high intelligence and many of the same behaviors

humans have, which is different than most animals.

4

What is the takeaway from this text? (Conclusion Part B)

We should treat humpback whales more humanely because they are a lot

like us. We should use OUR intelligence to realize this and stop killing them just

because we can. (per the author)

Humpback Whales:
ANNOTATED CONSTRUCTED RESPONSE EXEMPLAR

Prompt: What does the author **really** want us to know about humpback whales?

Note: The following annotated exemplar is aligned with the Constructed Response Instructional Rubric Grades 5–8 (pages 158–159) and the Constructed Response Student Checklist Grades 5–8 (page 160).

Grades 5–6

The author wants us to know that we share many human-like qualities with humpback whales and that these very qualities should make us think about treating them more **Ⓐ**humanely. "Humpback whales, like other whales, have been seen doing some very clever things." According to the text, humpback whales have even developed a way to communicate with one another. The ability to communicate is certainly thought of as a sign of intelligence, but actual language is thought of as a human quality. "People who have encountered humpbacks often say the whales even seemed to want to communicate with them." Communication is key to shared **Ⓑ**thoughts. Scientists have found that humpback brains "have a complex structure, or shape. The cortex, or outer part of the humpback brain, is deeply folded and made up of several layers, in a similar way to a human brain." Scientists have even found spindle cells, thought to be used in language and understanding emotions, in the brains of humpbacks. If the structure of a humpback's brain is similar to a human brain, perhaps humpback whales are capable of thinking **Ⓒ**similarly to humans. According to the author, humpbacks are also capable of learning and not just acting according to instinct like most other animals. "Like humans, humpbacks learn a lot as they grow up. Adult humpbacks also learn things from each other, such as new songs and new methods of hunting." In fact, one method of hunting used by humpbacks, bubble-net hunting, requires that the animals coordinate their efforts, communicate with one another, and cooperate to catch their prey. The text suggests that these abilities to share "social activities and creations" are a sign of the use of tools, further evidence that humpbacks share human qualities and **Ⓓ**abilities. Humans communicate, learn, share social activities, and make use of tools in everyday life, like humpbacks. It seems the qualities we share with humpbacks make us more alike than we might have **Ⓔ**thought. The author asks us to consider "should smart animals be treated better?" Should we treat humpbacks differently because they are "like us"? Maybe a sign of human intelligence would be a more humane treatment of humpback **Ⓕ**whales.

Ⓐ Answer/Thesis

Ⓑ Text Evidence #1 Interwoven with Rationale

Ⓒ Text Evidence #2 Interwoven with Rationale

Ⓓ Text Evidence #3 Interwoven with Rationale

Ⓔ Conclusion Part A

Ⓕ Conclusion Part B

THOUGHT CAPTURER GRADES 3–4

Name: _____

1 What does the author *really* want us to know about _____ ?
(answer/central idea)

_____

_____

_____

2 Which text evidence **most strongly** supports this answer/central idea?

Text Evidence	This is relevant because . . . (rationale)
• • •	• • •

3 How does your rationale connect to the answer/central idea? (Conclusion Part A)

_____

_____

_____

4 What is the takeaway from this text? (Conclusion Part B)

_____

_____

_____

THOUGHT CAPTURER GRADES 5–8

Name:_____

1 What does the author *really* want us to know about _____?
(answer/thesis)

_____

_____

_____

_____

2 Which text evidence **most strongly** supports this answer/thesis?

Text Evidence	This is relevant because . . . (rationale)
•	•
•	•
•	•

3 How does your rationale connect to the answer/thesis? (Conclusion Part A)

_____

_____

_____

_____

4 What is the takeaway from this text? (Conclusion Part B)

_____

_____

_____

_____

CONSTRUCTED RESPONSE
Instructional Rubrics and Student Checklists

Purpose

It is recommended that the Thought Capturer (pages 150–151) be used as a prewriting organizer to capture the essence of the facilitated discussion and to give students the opportunity to synthesize the key elements of the conversation in their own words before being asked to answer the prompt.

Constructed Response Instructional Rubrics, intended for teacher use, have been included for grades 3–4 and grades 5–8. They outline the elements of a constructed response and provide development gradations for assessing student performance from Emerging to Exceeding.

The Response to Reading Checklists mirror the gradation for Exceeding and are provided for student self-assessment and for direct feedback from the teacher.

Explanation
Constructed Response Instructional Rubric Elements Grades 3–4 Linked to Thought Capturer

1. Answer: must contain the central idea from the discussion.
2. Text Evidence: should support the answer and come from the Thought Capturer organizer section 2.
3. Rationale: should explain why text evidence supports the answer and come from the Thought Capturer organizer section 2.
4. Conclusion Part A: should demonstrate synthesis of the answer, text evidence, and rationale and come from the Thought Capturer organizer section 3.
5. Conclusion Part B: should include a "new idea" that logically flows from the logic and synthesis of the ideas in the constructed response and come from the Thought Capturer organizer section 4.
6. Language: should be used with discretion. Students should be encouraged to incorporate grade-appropriate conventions into their writing, but the emphasis of instruction, especially initially, should be on the transference of ideas from oral to written discourse.

Constructed Response Instructional Rubric Elements Grades 5–8 Linked to Thought Capturer

1. <u>Answer:</u> must contain a thesis based on the central idea from the discussion.

2. <u>Text Evidence:</u> should support the thesis and come from the Thought Capturer organizer section 2. Emphasis should be on the relevance of the evidence chosen. It should strongly support the thesis.

3. <u>Rationale:</u> should explain why text evidence supports the answer and come from the Thought Capturer organizer section 2. It should be interwoven with the text evidence to form the basis of the student's argument.

4. <u>Conclusion Part A:</u> should demonstrate synthesis of the answer, text evidence, and rationale and come from the Thought Capturer organizer section 3.

5. <u>Conclusion Part B:</u> should include a "new idea" that logically flows from the logic and synthesis of the ideas in the constructed response and come from the Thought Capturer organizer section 4.

6. <u>Argument:</u> should demonstrate an understanding of both the central idea and the ability to present a logical, clear, and convincing argument.

7. <u>Language:</u> should be used with discretion. Students should be encouraged to incorporate grade-appropriate conventions into their writing, but the emphasis of instruction, especially initially, should be on the transference of ideas from oral to written discourse.

Response to Reading Student Checklist Grades K–2

1. Aligned with Response to Reading worksheets specific to lessons
2. Includes space for teacher feedback and personal reflection

Response to Reading Student Checklist Grades 3–4

1. Aligned with Constructed Response Instructional Rubric
2. Includes space for teacher feedback and personal reflection

Response to Reading Student Checklist Grades 5–8

1. Aligned with Constructed Response Instructional Rubric
2. Includes space for teacher/peer feedback and personal reflection

RESPONSE TO READING CHECKLIST
Grades K–2

Name: _____

_____ **1** I followed the directions given.

_____ **2** I used words and/or pictures to show what I know.

_____ **3** I answered the question/s.

_____ **4** I explained what the text said.

_____ **5** My work shows that I understood the class discussion.

Teacher Feedback

What you did well:

_____

_____

_____

What needs some work:

_____

_____

_____

Personal Reflection

One thing to work on for next time:

_____

_____

_____

CONSTRUCTED RESPONSE
Instructional Rubric Grades 3–4

Common Core Anchor Standards:
Reading for Information #1 & #2,
Writing #9, and Language #1

ELEMENT	EMERGING *Student work is far below "Meeting" criteria.*	DEVELOPING *Student work contains some, but not all, of the "Meeting" requirements.*	MEETING *Student work includes all of the criteria listed below.*	EXCEEDING *Student work adds extended synthesis to "Meeting" criteria.*
Answer (contains central idea)	Missing from topic sentence or incorrect	**Implied** in topic sentence but not stated until the conclusion	**Clearly stated** in the topic sentence	Clearly and **thoughtfully stated** in the topic sentence
Text Evidence	Summarizes the text without answering the question	Limited, unconvincing, and/or irrelevant	**2 relevant** pieces that **support the answer**	**2 or more** relevant pieces that **strongly** support the answer
	Quotes missing and/or do not support the answer	Quotes are **list-like**, but support the answer	**Connection** between the quotes and the answer is evident	Connection between quotes and answer is **clearly stated and logical**
Rationale	Rationale explaining connection between the evidence and the answer is missing and/or insufficient	Some rationale is provided, but **inference is required** to make connections between the evidence and the answer	**Rationale provided** to explain connections between the evidence and the answer	**Thorough** rationale provided to explain connections between the evidence and the answer

CONSTRUCTED RESPONSE
Instructional Rubric Grades 3–4

Common Core Anchor Standards:
Reading for Information #1 & #2,
Writing #9, and Language #1

ELEMENT	EMERGING *Student work is far below "Meeting" criteria.*	DEVELOPING *Student work contains some, but not all, of the "Meeting" requirements.*	MEETING *Student work includes all of the criteria listed below.*	EXCEEDING *Student work adds extended synthesis to "Meeting" criteria.*
Conclusion Part A	Missing or unrelated to the answer	Connection to the answer is **implied** or **unclear**	**Simply restates** support of the answer and includes **the central idea**	**Synthesizes** support of the answer by **explaining its connection to the central idea**
Conclusion Part B	Missing or unrelated to the answer	Missing or unrelated to the author's point of view	Implied new idea stemming from synthesis of the author's point of view	Stated new idea stemming from synthesis of the author's point of view
Language	Significant mistakes in the conventions of standard English: Grammar Usage Capitalization Punctuation Spelling	**Some** mistakes in the conventions of standard English: Grammar Usage Capitalization Punctuation Spelling	**Few** mistakes in the conventions of standard English: Grammar Usage Capitalization Punctuation Spelling	**Demonstrates command** of the conventions of standard English: Grammar Usage Capitalization Punctuation Spelling

CONSTRUCTED RESPONSE
Student Checklist Grades 3–4

Name:_____

_____ **1** My answer is **stated in the topic sentence** and includes the **central idea of the text.**

_____ **2** I included at least **2 pieces of text evidence** to support my answer and **both** are **directly connected** to the **central idea of the text.**

_____ **3** I included a **rationale** to **explain why** the text evidence helps support my answer.

_____ **4** My conclusion restates my **answer**, my **support**, and the **central idea** using **different words** than I used in the rest of the paragraph.

_____ **5** I included a **new idea** in my conclusion that is my "aha" moment or takeaway from the text (something the author wanted me to think about after I'd read what he or she had to say).

_____ **6** I reread my whole answer **out loud**, and the **sentences, punctuation,** and **ideas** all **sound right** and **make sense.**

_____ **7** I checked my writing for conventions: **grammar, capitalization,** and **spelling.**

Teacher Feedback
Strengths:

_____

_____

_____

What needs work:

_____

_____

_____

Reflection
One thing I will concentrate on for next time:

_____

_____

_____

CONSTRUCTED RESPONSE
Instructional Rubric Grades 5–8

ELEMENT	EMERGING *Student work is far below "Meeting" criteria.*	DEVELOPING *Student work contains some, but not all, of the "Meeting" requirements.*	MEETING *Student work includes all of the criteria listed below.*	EXCEEDING *Student work adds extended synthesis to "Meeting" criteria.*
Answer (thesis)	Missing from topic sentence and/or does not answer the prompt	**Suggested** in topic sentence and/or included in the **conclusion only**	**Clearly stated** in the topic sentence	Clearly and **insightfully** stated in the topic sentence
Text Evidence	Summarizes the text without answering the question Quotes and paraphrasing are limited and/or do not support the answer	Limited, unconvincing, and/or irrelevant Quotes **or** paraphrasing is used, but seems **list-like** and/or **insufficient**	**3 relevant** pieces that **support thesis** **Balance** of specific quotes and paraphrased references to text	3 or more relevant pieces that **strongly** support thesis Balance of specific quotes and paraphrased references **interwoven with rationale**
Rationale	Rationale explaining connection between the evidence and the thesis is missing and/or unclear	Some rationale is provided, but **inference is required** to make connections between the evidence and the thesis	**Rationale provided** to explain connections between the evidence and the thesis	Thorough rationale provided to explain connections between the evidence, the thesis, and **the argument**

CONSTRUCTED RESPONSE
Instructional Rubric Grades 5–8

ELEMENT	EMERGING *Student work is far below "Meeting" criteria.*	DEVELOPING *Student work contains some, but not all, of the "Meeting" requirements.*	MEETING *Student work includes all of the criteria listed below.*	EXCEEDING *Student work adds extended synthesis to "Meeting" criteria.*
Conclusion Part A	Missing or unrelated to the thesis New idea is missing or is irrelevant	Restatement of topic sentence and/or connection to the thesis is **implied** or **unclear**	**Synthesizes** text evidence and rationale and **explains** connection to the thesis	**Insightfully** synthesizes text evidence and rationale and connection to the thesis is **clearly** explained
Conclusion Part B		New idea comes directly **from the text**, is **implied**, and/or is **illogical**	New idea is drawn from **author's point of view** and is **clearly stated**	New idea is an **inferred extension of the central idea**
Argument	Indicates misconceptions and/or limited understanding of the text Not validated by text evidence Contains **illogical** and/or **incomplete** reasoning Does not reflect author's point of view	**Implies understanding** of the central ideas in the text, but **requires inference** **Validation** by text evidence is **limited** Contains **flaws** in reasoning **Partially reflects** the author's point of view	**Demonstrates** understanding of the central ideas in the text **Validated** by text evidence **Clear** reasoning **Reflects** the author's point of view	Demonstrates **deep** understanding of the central ideas in the text **Solidly** validated by text evidence Clear and **convincing** reasoning **Strongly** reflects the author's point of view
Language	**Significant** mistakes in the conventions of standard English: Grammar Usage Capitalization Punctuation Spelling	**Some** mistakes in the conventions of standard English: Grammar Usage Capitalization Punctuation Spelling	**Few** mistakes in the conventions of standard English: Grammar Usage Capitalization Punctuation Spelling	**Demonstrates command** of the conventions of standard English: Grammar Usage Capitalization Punctuation Spelling

CONSTRUCTED RESPONSE
Student Checklist Grades 5–8

Name:_____

_____ 1. My thesis is stated in the **topic sentence** and contains the **central idea** of the text.

_____ 2. I included 3 **relevant** pieces of text evidence to **support** my thesis.

_____ 3. I used **both** quotes and paraphrasing to **validate** my argument.

_____ 4. I included **sufficient rationale** for the reader to understand the **connection** between my thesis, my text evidence, and the **logic of my argument.**

_____ 5. My conclusion is a **synthesis** of what I am saying about the central idea of the text.

_____ 6. My conclusion contains a **new idea** that grew out of the central idea and came from my close analysis of the **author's point of view.**

_____ 7. My argument **shows** that I understand the central ideas in the text.

_____ 8. The **text evidence** I chose not only supports my thesis, but also **validates my argument.**

_____ 9. I presented **clear reasoning** (the reader doesn't have to figure anything out).

_____ 10. My writing reflects the **author's point of view**, not my own.

_____ 11. I reread my writing out loud and it **sounds right** and **makes sense.**

_____ 12. I **edited** my writing for conventions: capitalization, punctuation, and spelling.

Teacher/Peer Feedback
Strengths:

_____

_____

_____

What needs work:

_____

_____

_____

Reflection
One thing to work on for next time based on feedback:

_____

_____

_____

GLOSSARY

academic vocabulary: refers to words used in academic dialogue and text that form the language of learning across domains from K–12. For example: concept words, such as *observe, create,* and *similar;* and signal words, such as *indeed, hence, although,* and *therefore*

annotate: to supply with explanatory notes; for example, each Teacher Discussion Guide includes annotated lessons to facilitate lesson delivery

answer: to supply a thoughtful response to a question or prompt supported by text evidence

argument: the point an author or writer presents to the reader using evidence to support a specific position

CCSS: Common Core State Standards were established to provide a consistent set of expectations for what students are expected to learn at specific points in their educational careers in order to prepare them for college and careers by the end of twelfth grade

central idea: what the author really wants you to know about a given topic. There can be more than one suggested by the text

conclusion: a summary of the reasoning process; a statement that follows logically from others presented

constructed response: an assessment that asks students to apply knowledge, skills, and critical thinking abilities to standards-driven performance tasks requiring students to "construct" or develop their own answers based on text evidence

discussion: to share ideas by comment or through argument in speech or in writing

exemplar: a writing example included to show an excellent model of ultimate writing achievement for specific grade levels; aligned to the Exceeding gradation of the instructional rubrics

explicit: very clearly stated, leaving no question as to meaning

facilitation: to assist in the understanding of a process, such as the facilitation of discussion via a suggested set of questions

gist: a quick summary of the essential details rather than a thorough analysis

implicit: implied, not plainly expressed so as to require inference

informational text: nonfiction resources, including biographies, autobiographies, books about history, social studies, science, the arts, technical texts, and literary nonfiction

interwoven: to weave or blend ideas together, combining text evidence and rationale to support a thought

main idea: the key concept being expressed

new idea: a new thought developed or arrived at resulting from synthesis of the text or argument

partner(s): a person or people to share ideas or activities with

prompt: an open-ended question designed to elicit a thoughtful written response

rationale: a reason given to support text evidence; the "why you think so" part of a written piece

share out: the act of sharing one's ideas in an informal public way, in a group or classroom

small group: a collaborative gathering of 3–4 participants

student text: reproducible passage used as the basis of each close reading lesson

synthesis: the combination of separate elements to form a coherent whole (the "heart" of close reading)

Teacher Discussion Guide: annotated guide to facilitated discussion of the Student Text included with each lesson; scaffolded for differentiation

text: the words that make up the informational passages chosen for the close reading lessons

text-dependent questions: questions that can only be answered with evidence from the text

text evidence: words from a text that are used to support an answer

thesis: the main point or claim of a written work

Thought Capturer: organizer for capturing the essence of the discussion and for transfer of thought from verbal to written discourse; a prewriting organizer for answering the constructed response prompt that is integral to each lesson

turn and talk: a strategy used to elicit sharing of ideas about a topic, turning to another person and expressing one's thoughts in a verbal exchange

MASTER LIST OF CAPSTONE MENTOR TEXTS

Lesson texts were abridged and excerpted from the following Capstone publications with permission from the publishers.

Amstutz, Lisa J. *What Eats What in a Rain Forest Food Chain.* North Mankato, MN: Picture Window, 2013. Print.

Barber, Nicola. *Tomb Explorers.* Chicago, IL: Capstone Raintree, 2013. Print.

Claybourne, Anna. *Humpback Whales.* Chicago, IL: Heinemann Library, 2013. Print.

Dell, Pamela. *Man on the Moon: How a Photograph Made Anything Seem Possible.* North Mankato, MN: Compass Point, 2011. Print.

Hunt, Jilly. *Ethics of Politics: Leaders.* Chicago, IL: Heinemann Library, 2013. Print.

Hunter, Nick. *Ethics of Sports: Sportsmanship.* Chicago, IL: Heinemann Library, 2012. Print.

Lepetit, Angie. *Three Cheers for Trees!: A Book about Our Carbon Footprint.* North Mankato, MN: Capstone, 2013. Print.

Meister, Cari. *Everyone Feels Angry Sometimes.* North Mankato, MN: Capstone, 2010. Print.

Nardo, Don. *Mesopotamia.* North Mankato, MN: Compass Point, 2013. Print.

Rau, Dana Meachen. *Albert Einstein.* Minneapolis, MN: Compass Point, 2003. Print.

Slade, Suzanne. *What If There Were No Sea Otters?: A Book about the Ocean Ecosystem.* North Mankato, MN: Picture Window, 2011. Print.

Weil, Ann. *Medgar Evers.* Chicago, IL: Heinemann Library, 2013. Print.

At Maupin House by Capstone Professional, we continue to look for professional development resources that support grades K–8 classroom teachers in areas, such as these:

Literacy	Language Arts
Content-Area Literacy	Research-Based Practices
Assessment	Inquiry
Technology	Differentiation
Standards-Based Instruction	School Safety
Classroom Management	School Community

If you have an idea for a professional development resource, visit our Become an Author website at:

http://maupinhouse.com/index.php/become-an-author

There are two ways to submit questions and proposals.

1. You may send them electronically to:
   http://maupinhouse.com/index.php/become-an-author

2. You may send them via postal mail. Please be sure to include a self-addressed stamped envelope for us to return materials.

Acquisitions Editor
Capstone Professional
1 N. LaSalle Street, Suite 1800
Chicago, IL 60602